ALSO BY KATHERINE WHITESIDE AND MICK HALES

Antique Flowers

CLASSIC BULBS

CLASSIC BULBS

Hidden Treasures for the Modern Garden

By Katherine Whiteside   Photography by Mick Hales

With Forewords by Penelope Hobhouse and John Fitzpatrick

VILLARD BOOKS ❧ NEW YORK ❧ 1991

Early spring in the Hudson River Valley. Dried rhizomes of native American Bloodroot (Sanguinaria canadensis) were once used medicinally.

Text copyright © 1991 by Katherine Whiteside

Photographs copyright © 1991 by Mick Hales

Published in the United States by Villard Books, a division of Random House, Inc., New York, and simultaneously in Canada by Random House of Canada Limited, Toronto.

Villard Books is a registered trademark of Random House, Inc.

Library of Congress Cataloging-in-Publication Data

Whiteside, Katherine

   Classic bulbs: hidden treasures for the modern garden/by Katherine Whiteside: photography by Mick Hales.—1st ed.

    p. cm.

   Includes bibliographical references and index.

   ISBN 0-394-58727-8

   1. Bulbs—Heirloom varieties. 2. Bulbs. 3. Bulbs—Pictorial works. I. Hales, Michael. II. Title.

SB425.W56 1992

635.9′44—dc20   91-13956

Book design by Chris Welch

Manufactured in the United States of America

9 8 7 6 5 4 3 2

First Edition

Page ii: *Winter bulb-forcing at the Cloisters, a branch of the Metropolitan Museum of Art, in New York City.*

Page iv: *Summer lilies in the gardens designed by Penelope Hobhouse at Tintinhull in Somerset, England.*

Overleaf: *Callas were a popular Art Deco motif.*

Opposite: *The Whiteside–Hales garden in early June.*

This book is dedicated to Micah Devon Hales
and August Somerset Hales

ACKNOWLEDGMENTS

We would like to thank the following people and organizations for help with this book:

ALISON ACKER
ANDERSEN HORTICULTURAL LIBRARY
BEATRICE TOSTI
JEFFERY BEAM
EMILY BESTLER
CAROLINE BURGESS
FLORA ANN BYNUM
MADISON COX
DR. AUGUST A. DE HERTOGH
GEKE EISINGA
TOM FIFFER
JOHN FITZPATRICK
THE FORTY-FOUR MARKET STREET GANG
SALLY FERGUSON AND DAVID CARAS
PHYLLIS FYLES
NANCY GOODWIN
CON AND DULCE HALES
KEITH AND MARY HALES
BECKY AND BRENT HEATH
PENELOPE HOBHOUSE
KEN KIPPS
ALLEN LACY
BETTY LUBER
JIM MASSEY
SUSAN TAYLOR MOODY
NETHERLANDS FLOWER BULB INFORMATION CENTER
PEGGY NEWCOMB
LOUISE NOTMAN
THE ORDER OF THE BLACK TULIP
HELEN PRATT
ROSE QUALLEY
MARK REEDER
ROXANNE RITACCO
JANE ROBIE
FRANS ROOZEN
TONY SKITTONE
MARCO POLO STUFANO
CHRIS WELCH
HARRY AND BECKY WHITESIDE
TOM WHITESIDE
AMANDA WHITNEY

We would also like to thank the following people and organizations for allowing us to photograph their gardens:

SUZANNE BALES
RICHARD BATTENFELD
BROOKLYN BOTANIC GARDEN
ANNE AND FRANK CABOT
THE CLOISTERS
COLONIAL WILLIAMSBURG FOUNDATION
JAN COWLES
THE DAFFODIL MART
ROBERT DASH
EDITH EDDLEMAN
FEARRINGTON VILLAGE
CHRIS AND MIM GALLIGAN
PENNY HARRIS
PENELOPE HOBHOUSE
THE HUNNEWELL ESTATE
WILLIAM LANIER HUNT
JONES' WOOD GARDEN MEMBERS
LONGWOOD GARDENS
MONTICELLO: THOMAS JEFFERSON MEMORIAL
    FOUNDATION
MONTROSE NURSERY
EMMA MORGAN
NORTH CAROLINA STATE UNIVERSITY ARBORETUM
OLD SALEM
JENNY AND MARTIN QUARLES
OSCAR DE LA RENTA
NANCY AND TURNER REUTER
RENNY REYNOLDS
ELIZABETH AND ANDY ROCCHIA
DOUG RUHREN
SAINT GAUDENS NATIONAL HISTORIC SITE
GERALDINE STUTZ
THE TAVARES FAMILY
MICHAEL AND LADY ANNE TREE
BARONESS LOUISE DE WALDNER
WAVE HILL
WING HAVEN
WINTERTHUR
ABBIE ZABAR

FOREWORD

❧

The second half of the sixteenth century witnessed a novel and extraordinary influx of plants into European gardens. What looked like "unpromising onion-like bulbs and knobbly tubers" actually, as Professor Stearne described in his lecture, "brought forth tulips, crown imperials, irises, hyacinths, anemones, turban ranunculi, narcissi and lilies" to dazzle gardeners and delight botanists—and even, as Katherine Whiteside reminds us here, encouraged dishonorable trading in stolen garden rarities. For a gardener, all stories of plant discoveries stir the heart, but particularly engrossing are the tales of the dangers and deprivations suffered by intrepid plant hunters through the centuries. Many bulbs have been with us for hundreds of years, but it is sometimes difficult to remember that some of our most treasured garden bulbs have been grown in the West for only a short time. The Madonna Lily *(Lilium candidum)*, of uncertain origin but from somewhere around the eastern end of the Mediterranean, has been known almost since garden history was first recorded. Rather unromantically the Roman legions are supposed to have made an ointment from its bulbs to treat their corns, and for early Christians this lily symbolized the Virgin Mary with the white petals expressing the purity of her body, the golden anthers the glowing light of her soul. Other lilies, though, are of much more recent introduction. In our own century, Ernest H. ("Chinese") Wilson, perhaps the most successful of the great plant explorers, a man with an all-seeing eye for those plants most likely to prove garden-worthy, collected the Regal Lily *(Lilium regale)* in 1910 in the high mountains of

Dusty pink alliums in a summer border designed by Penelope Hobhouse at Tintinhull in Somerset, England.

western China. At the cost of almost losing his life—one of his legs was broken in an avalanche—Wilson, with the assistance of his native diggers and packers, introduced hundreds of the lily bulbs he found on this expedition by getting them safely back to Boston's Arnold Arboretum for distribution to gardeners. It seems almost incredible that the famous Gertrude Jekyll only had use of so magnificent and reliable a lily for her border schemes during the latter part of her life—all thanks to Mr. Wilson.

The colorful bulbs brought from Constantinople in the 1560s and '70s (often at that time already garden

❧

cultivars and not true wild species), as well as many others through the ensuing four hundred years, have been selected and "bred" to give us the modern nursery-grown plants that we can choose from illustrated catalogs. These are the "classic" bulbs that Katherine Whiteside describes so joyfully and Mick Hales illustrates with superb photography in this book. But the point of *Classic Bulbs* is that she goes much further than mere catalog descriptions. In tracing bulb ancestry and the story of how bulbs have been planted in the gardens of the West, the book is far-reaching and can be studied as a preparation before ordering and planting; it is full of historical anecdotes and incidents that add a dimension to the pleasures of growing.

But *Classic Bulbs* is not only a history book; it is a practical do-it-yourself guide with inspiring suggestions for planting and maintenance. It includes warnings concerning the dangers of buying from sources other than those that strictly adhere to the "no digging in the wild" code, and gives a welcome list of approved suppliers. In short, it is a primer for the gardener who will be satisfied with nothing less than the best—bulbous plants that add beauty, interest, and history to the garden while leaving nature's wild garden intact.

PENELOPE HOBHOUSE
Tintinhull House
Somerset, England

Showy flowering bulbs were prominent in early American pleasure gardens. At least forty species arrived before the Revolution, including some of today's familiar spring favorites—tulips, hyacinths, and daffodils. Then as now, growing bulbs was easy: they could be transported across the Atlantic more dependably than live herbaceous plants, and growing them successfully, unlike many kinds of seeds, didn't require trained gardeners. Neither advantage was lost on colonial gardeners, for whom shipping added a remarkable element of challenge. Shipping difficulties were well known to John Custis of Williamsburg, who exchanged plants with Peter Collinson of London between 1734 and 1746. Custis found that the long voyages and unavoidable delays, the abundance of rats and shortage of fresh water on board the ships, and the crew's inattention to plant cargo all worked against the delivery of living plants. He quickly gave up on asking for herbaceous plants, but received at least eleven kinds of bulbs, including three you will read about in *Classic Bulbs*—Spring Cyclamen, Sternbergia, and Crown Imperial.

Just ten years after the Revolution the fashion for bulbs was in full bloom and hundreds of varieties were available to American gardeners. A traveling salesman for Peter Crouwells and Co. of Philadelphia advertised his seeds and bulbs in the *Virginia Journal & Alexandria Advertiser* in April of that year. The list included an astounding six hundred Poppy Anemones, four hundred Turban Ranunculuses, six hundred Dutch Hyacinths, and four hundred Tulip varieties. Only a handful of them still exist.

In October 1792, Minton Collins of Richmond, Virginia, advertised that he had "just received from London, in the ship *Bowman* . . . a choice collection of FLOWER ROOTS, which are warranted to be of the last summer's growth," including the four prominent species offered by Crouwells, plus bulbs of Persian Iris, Tazetta Narcissus, Tuberose, crocuses in blue and yellow, Belladonna Lily, and "some white glass bottles to hold the flower roots." Bulbs produced in Europe and containers for forcing them into bloom had become established features of the American marketplace.

Starting in the 1790s, Thomas Jefferson was able to include these same fashionable bulbs in his flower garden at Monticello. The striped and Parrot tulips held a strong appeal for his grandchildren, one of whom recollected the eagerness with which they went out on spring mornings to see which were appearing. Between 1807 and 1817, Jefferson added bulbs recently introduced from the Cape of Good Hope, including *Chasmanthe aethiopica* (included in this book), *Tritonia hyalina,* and *Watsonia meriana*. In the decade after Jefferson's death in 1826, transatlantic steamships and the prosperity of the young nation assured that supplies of the newest, most exotic bulbs would be available to American gardeners.

Classic Bulbs is a celebration of these plants as part of our cultural heritage and, *ipso facto,* a call for their pres-

Solomon's Seal grows in the restored garden of Monticello, Thomas Jefferson's home, where John Fitzpatrick is director of The Center for Historic Plants.

ervation. Hundreds of varieties of garden origins have been lost through neglect and the relentless pursuit of novelty. However, dedicated gardeners have saved a handful of the older bulbs, and today, dozens of historic gardens around the country, such as Monticello, seek older bulb varieties for authentic period gardens. From these sanctuaries, neglected older varieties can be reintroduced. For the many people developing period gardens, Katherine Whiteside offers a selection of garden-worthy bulbs from which to choose. Not content just to support the preservation of cultivated varieties, she also takes a clear stand against the collection of flower bulbs in the wild, which threatens the survival of some species.

But *Classic Bulbs* goes way beyond the bulbs of our forefathers to include a wide range of varieties that can provide year-round garden interest, from the most venerable, such as Meadow Saffron, Madonna Lily, and Egyptian Walking Onion, to more recent introductions, such as Gold-banded Lily (1862), 'King Alfred' Daffodil (1899), and the fragrant Night-blooming Daylily (about 1902). Katherine Whiteside shares her own delight and that of her children in growing these bulbs—whether for indoor bulb extravaganzas or in tiny garden beds chock full of crocuses and species tulips.

Whiteside uses the word, "bulbs" in its broadest vernacular sense: to include plants with underground storage organs variously called corms, tubers, rhizomes, bulbs, and fleshy storage roots. While *Classic Bulbs* is thoroughly researched and technically accurate, it is never academic or dry. It draws on the words and ideas of a host of respected garden writers from John Gerard to E. A. Bowles and Louise Beebe Wilder, but doesn't hesitate to express a contrary opinion now and then.

Each article is headed with the name of the genus and family, followed by the botanical and common names of the species included. Botanical names follow the standard reference, *Hortus Third.* Throughout the book, common names for specific varieties appear with initial capitals for clarity, while references to several species are in lower case. Thus you will read of lilies and crocuses, but Martagon Lily and Saffron Crocus.

Katherine Whiteside's narratives are enhanced by the exceptional photographs taken by Mick Hales. Like the best family snapshots, these professional photographs capture the individual beauty and character of each plant. I get a sense of actually looking through his camera lens and seeing the gardens where these heirloom bulbs grow. They look like places where regular dirt-under-the-fingernails gardeners are creating and maintaining their own little corners of paradise.

Classic Bulbs is a practical guide to using bulbs indoors and out. It describes and recommends methods that have proved successful, proposing a multitude of possibilities, rather than dictating exactly how, when, or where readers should grow them. I encourage you to step in wherever the photographs look most inviting and sample the delights of Katherine Whiteside's sometimes irreverent, always animated and informed, essays on her favorite classic bulbs.

JOHN T. FITZPATRICK
Monticello
Charlottesville, Virginia

CONTENTS

❧

FOREWORD BY PENELOPE HOBHOUSE *ix*

FOREWORD BY JOHN T. FITZPATRICK *x*

INTRODUCTION *xvii*

Acidanthera: Iridaceae *2*

Allium: Amaryllidaceae *6*

Anemone: Ranunculaceae *14*

Begonia: Begoniaceae *20*

Caladium: Araceae *26*

Canna: Cannaceae *30*

Chasmanthe: Iridaceae *34*

Bluebells in the woods at Wing Haven in Charlotte, North Carolina.

xiii

❧

Colchicum: Liliaceae   *36*

Colocasia: Araceae   *42*

Crocus: Iridaceae   *44*

Cyclamen: Primulaceae   *52*

Fritillaria: Liliaceae   *58*

Hermerocallis: Liliaceae   *62*

Hyacinthus: Liliaceae   *70*

Iris: Iridaceae   *76*

Lilium: Liliaceae   *88*

Overleaf: Trillium erectum *growing wild in the Hudson River Valley.*

The soft autumn foliage of Solomon's Seal (**Polygonatum** *sp.*).

Lycoris: Amaryllidaceae   *98*

Melasphaerula: Iridaceae   *102*

Muscari: Liliaceae   *104*

Narcissus: Amaryllidaceae   *108*

Oxalis: Oxalidaceae   *120*

Puschkinia: Liliaceae   *122*

Scilla: Liliaceae   *126*

Sternbergia: Amaryllidaceae   *130*

Tulipa: Liliaceae   *136*

Zantedeschia: Araceae   *148*

SOURCES   *157*
Where to Find the Flowers   *157*
Nurseries   *161*

BIBLIOGRAPHY   *167*
USDA PLANT HARDINESS ZONE MAP   *173*
INDEX   *175*

INTRODUCTION

Clean and round,
Heavy and sound,
In every bulb a flower.

Life would be so dull without a few mysteries, and the inscrutable flower bulb has been entertaining mankind for eons. What a leap of faith—to bury a funny brown stone and wait for it to spring forth with green leaves and a colorful, perfumed flower. But bulbs must be a kind of magic that we all believe in, because the popularity of these easy-to-grow and wonderful-to-show plants increases yearly by leaps and bounds.

No matter what your level of gardening experience, *Classic Bulbs* is the book for you. Our first book, *Antique Flowers,* was dedicated to gardeners who wanted beautiful, easy, old-fashioned flowers to satisfy their increasingly sophisticated garden tastes. Now you can adorn your garden with another bookload of plants that promises you old favorites like daffodils and lilies, plus a few venerable surprises like begonias and caladiums. *Classic Bulbs* makes it so simple and fun that even a stark, raving amateur will find everything necessary for adding four (and maybe even five) seasons of bulb pleasure to the garden.

As you flip through this book you will spot many gorgeous flowers that don't necessarily seem like bulbs.

Wave Hill's exuberant autumn garden includes many bulbous plants such as Tuberoses (almost ready to bloom in foreground) and red dahlias.

A jumble of narcissus and tulip bulbs ready for planting.

Actually, a crocus comes from a corm, some irises arise from rhizomes, but *Hortus Third* allows them, and others, to be loosely classified as bulbs. *Hortus Third* has decreed: "When defined as a horticultural class, bulbs are ornamental, partial season, mostly simple-stemmed plants arising from bulbs, corms, tubers, or thickened rhizomes." This definition saves us from having to deal with the rather weighty title *Beautiful Bulbs, Classic Corms, Terrific Tubers, and Ravishing Rhizomes.* There is a modern movement toward renaming the admittedly catchall term "bulbs" and calling all these underground-

Onions, members of the Lily Family, are edible bulbs.

storehouse-type plants "geophytes," but let's just hope this doesn't catch on too fast. It would be awful to have to update this title and call it *Good Old Geophytes*.

But whether the plant in question is a corm, tuber, or whatever, all the bulbous plants in this book (and in the world) have one shared, sterling characteristic: they solve the eternal environmental problem known as Bad Weather. When everything in the outside world is sublimely perfect—right amount of water, right amount of sun, nice comfortable temperature—a bulbous plant is like the industrious ant of the old fable. It works! Not only does it flower, but a bulb also makes leaves that allow energy (in the form of starch) to be stored in personal "Clean and round/ Heavy and sound" banks underground. Then, when Bad Weather strikes, whether it comes as ice and snow or heat and drought, your bulb can retreat into its underground shelter. There it is able to stay alive, but dormant, for relatively long periods of adverse conditions. Then, as soon as good weather returns, so do your flowers.

So if underground storehouses make a bulb, what makes a classic? The answer lies in the fact that bulbs and mankind go way back. From very early times, people realized that bulbs had special properties that were at once useful, fascinating, and endearing. Bulbous plants, such as alliums, for instance, were highly regarded as food and medicine, they were easy to carry around, and last, but far from least, they had that aforementioned magical property of suddenly springing forth with beautiful flowers. We know that bulb fanatics date back at least to the Bronze Age, because ancient Minoan artisans drew recognizable tulips on their wonderful vases and frescoes. All throughout recorded history, everyone from householders, soldiers, sailors, traders, merchants, herbalists, writers, crusaders, right down to thieves and rapscallions found one bulb or another of those included in this book to take to heart.

Renny Reynolds's garden on Long Island. This traditional American spring garden includes bulbs from all over the world.

Because of that wonderful dormant period when the plant retreats into its bulb, these plants traveled around long before other annuals and perennials did. Whether wrapped in pieces of precious silk and royally transported in embroidered pouches or rudely thrust into a rough sack with other basic wayfaring victuals, bulbs moved readily from one end of the earth to the other. Daylilies arrived in Europe at a very early date by way of the overland spice routes, while some narcissuses made their way eastward, from the region we now call Spain, into India, and even farther, on to China. Soldiers of the Roman Empire spread bulbs around their far-flung posts, and twelfth-century Crusaders brought bulbs from the Holy Land back to western Europe.

Given this enormous chunk of history, just about any bulb that endures to this day can safely be called a classic. Some included here were grown by Middle Age monks, others were brought from South Africa two centuries ago, while some, such as that wonderful daffodil 'King Alfred', have yet to make their hundredth. Classic bulbs are nothing more than the long-loved, traditional treasures of the garden.

Fascinating history aside, the modern gardener grows bulbs because they give four (and even five) seasons of pleasure. Somehow, the mistaken notion that bulbs are just for spring once slipped into the great gardening subconscious, but this is a fallacy that is exploded with the very first flower in *Classic Bulbs*. The shimmering white Acidanthera is one of the real treats of autumn, and joins those devilish Naked Boys and Spider Lilies of the old South to make fall a whole new garden sea-

Anemones have worked their
magic in the hearts of
gardeners for centuries.

Crocus corms and favorite books from the author's collection.

son. There are also June's proud ranks of irises, followed by the planting-out time for the Never-Say-Never series of wonderful bulbous plants: the cannas, caladiums, and colocasias that tempt the temperate gardener to explore new ways with old tropicals. Mild winters in California and the Deep South have irises, alliums, crocuses, and puschkinias blooming during the time that the rest of the country deals with ice and snow. Yet bulbs offer frozen-land gardeners what will here be called the Fifth Season.

Forcing bulbs for indoor flowering is certainly nothing new. The ancient Romans encouraged bulbs into early bloom indoors, Philip Miller—who ran the venerable Chelsea Physic Garden for most of the eighteenth century—forced bulbs under glass, and the Victorians later raised this horticultural experiment to the fine art of parlor gardening. Bulbs make ideal houseplants, and whereas there is much fickleness involved with germinating seeds, almost any dormant bulb can be tricked into producing roots, leaves, and flowers once its ideal life-style has been ascertained.

Classic Bulbs gives detailed instructions for forcing dainty Roman Hyacinths, headily perfumed Chinese Sacred Lilies, and the surprisingly stately Chasmanthe. Now you can move far beyond the rather shopworn Paperwhite into the world of windowsill pots of species tulips and fantastic indoor crocus gardens. All the bulbs included here are just about foolproof, and once you've tried them you can fine-tune your indoor garden to include month after month of bloom. Pots of cheery bulbs

Englishman John Parkinson grew Trout Lily collected during New World explorations in the 1600s. Today, wild collection of this, or any bulbous plant, is not acceptable. Photographed in the wild in the Hudson River Valley.

are the nicest way to lighten up the raw, bitter days of winter; the Fifth Season may become your favorite.

In among all the plants included here are the names and words of familiar old garden writers. Everyone from first-century naturalist Pliny to late-sixteenth- and early-seventeenth-century plant lovers like Clusius, Gerard, and Parkinson and right up to beloved authors of the last century—Robinson, Bowles, Lawrence, and Wilder—gets a chance to promote his or her favorite bulbs. If you sometimes have a hard time remembering who is who, just check the index for further biographical information. You'll find that certain names will pop up throughout *Classic Bulbs* like familiar tunes in an opera. These authors, like the plants they write about, are the enduring classics everyone knows and loves.

Because you're not really any different from the householders, soldiers, traders, herbalists, and rapscallions of yore, you're bound to fall in love with at least one bulb in this book. Fortunately, getting hold of your desired treasure is going to be as easy as consulting the Sources section at the back of the book. Each praiseworthy plant included in *Classic Bulbs* is available by mail order, and where possible several nurseries are listed. Whereas it once would have involved a long journey by camel and many gold pieces, gathering bulbs today involves merely licking a stamp and writing a check.

But speaking of gathering your bulbs, please do be sensible and refuse to buy bulbs collected in the wild. Thanks to recent legislation, this senseless practice will

The final stages of winter
bulb-forcing at the Whiteside–
Hales home takes place on
the dining room table.

The aptly named Snowdrop
in the author's
Hoboken garden.

Lily-of-the-valley, a famed
perfumer indoors and out,
was an important medieval
medicinal plant.

One of summer's offerings to the bulb world is the stately iris, here at Baroness de Waldner's garden in the south of France.

soon, we hope, become part of the deep, dark past. But until it does, be sure to ask your supplier *not* to send you bulbs collected in the wild. Indiscriminate collecting is as selfish a practice as littering—but, of course, you don't do that either.

That little warning heeded, you are now ready to dig into the wonderful world of bulbs. No matter where and how you garden, *Classic Bulbs* is going to change the way you think about plants. Because no matter how sophisticated you get, there's something downright enchanted about burying little treasure chests and waiting for them to pop open with flowers. It's nothing less than magic.

CLASSIC BULBS

Acidanthera: Iridaceae

୨ଈ

A. BICOLOR—PEACOCK ORCHID, MAGPIE GLADIOLUS

*I*t is great fun to start the portraits with Acidanthera—a wonderful flower that immediately breaks the only-for-spring stereotype so often associated with bulbous plants. This gracefully tall, scented white flower brings a new thrill to late summer and autumn, reminding the gardener that there is, indeed, reason to live after July.

A vigorous Acidanthera may reach three feet tall. Its flowers are attached to the stalk with a gracefully curved, sometimes slightly pinkish neck, better called a perianth tube. Acidanthera blossoms are sulfur-white, and open wide, like lilies. The fragrant flowers are about three inches across, and the three lower petals have a spot of color at their bases ranging from chocolate brown to brownish purple. It may come as a surprise that the graceful, serene Acidanthera is the center of controversy for those who like to fight over nomenclature.

Some experts consider *Acidanthera bicolor* just another member of the large *Gladiolus* clan and rechristen it *Gladiolus callianthus. Acidanthera* and *Gladiolus* are distinct genera ("genera" is the plural of "genus"). The genus *Gladiolus* has about 300 species and has many, many cultivated varieties (cultivars) available. Although the genus *Acidanthera* has about thirty-three species, the only one in general cultivation is *A. bicolor.* (The name of a species consists of two words. The first is the name of the genus—or the generic name—and the second, technically called the specific epithet, identifies the exact genus member.)

But in the case of this lovely flower, the experts just can't seem to agree whether to call it *Acidanthera bicolor* or *Gladiolus callianthus,* sending researchers zinging back and forth between A and G, with no official stopping place in sight.

In his authoritative two-volume work on bulbs, American expert John Bryan sidesteps the *Acidanthera*

At the Cabot garden in Murray Bay, Canada, graceful **Acidanthera bicolor** *is one of the glories of autumn.*

Overleaf: *Tiny scillas pack a subtle blue punch at the Hunnewell estate in Boston.*

or *Gladiolus* issue a bit, but seems to include the plant under the genus *Gladiolus.* Graham Stuart Thomas, Gardens Consultant of the National Trust of England and author of the highly respected *Perennial Garden Plants,* also calls this plant *G. callianthus.* However, *Hortus Third,* the gardener's and horticulturist's reference to cultivated species in North America, takes another approach. *Hortus Third* says this plant should be called *A. bicolor,* not *G. callianthus,* because that swanlike neck is actually straight, or essentially so; its curve is caused only by the weight of the corolla. Acidantheras, according to *Hortus Third,* are a straight-necked bunch and gladioluses are decidedly bent. But despite this lucid argument, everyone still does not agree.

The absolute unofficial, opinionated, and emotional decision made here is that this plant must be considered *Acidanthera* because *Gladiolus* has many flowers commonly in cultivation and *Acidanthera* has only this one. This should end this nomenclature discussion, except that many books and catalogues include *A. b.* var. *mu-*

rielae as a distinct species, though *Hortus* says that this further complication is "a listed name of no botanical standing." The point is, do look up and order this flower under any or all of these names, call it what you wish, argue about it if you desire, but until further notice, Acidanthera is its name here.

Most sources agree that *Acidanthera bicolor* was introduced in 1896, and everyone recognizes that the name arises from the Greek *akis* "pointed" and Latin *anthera* "anther." (The anther, which bears the pollen, is the business end of the stamen.) Everyone also agrees that this is a wonderful, under-utilized bulbous plant (technically a corm) that will grow very well in just about every region of the United States and England.

In zones 8 through 11 this East African native can stay in the ground year round. The South of France and Southern California both could be Acidanthera heaven, because the plant does not require lots of water. Seven is a bit risky, so winter mulching is essential. (Refer to the USDA Hardiness Zone Map on page 173.)

However, everyone up to zone 3 (Canada) can enjoy the autumnal delights of Acidantheras if they are ready to partake in the most pleasant ritual of between-frosts gardening. Plant the corms after the last spring frost (April or May), enjoy the flowers in September and October, and dig them back up before the first frost. (Watch the newspapers.) Gently lift the Acidanthera corms out of the soil with a garden fork and let them dry for a day or two. Then brush the earth off, taking care not to disturb the corms' outer layers. After you have dried and cleaned the Acidanthera harvest, it is recommended that you store the corms in a dry spot between 60 and 68 degrees—which means you can keep them in a clothes closet where mice and other corm gourmets are unlikely to venture. Margery Fish believed that keeping the corms warm would help those in England to bring their flowers into full bloom the following season. Unfortunately her experiments with this method were foiled by a "hungry little mouse."

Acidantheras are striking on their own, and make stunning, fragrant plants for large tubs. They also make a bright addition to the late-summer and autumn border. Be sure to plant them someplace where they can be admired in the cool evenings of early autumn. At that time, their starry white flowers will shine in the gold tones of the lowering sun, and if one is lucky, their sweet beauty will successfully attract a hawkmoth (Acidanthera's pollinator) to hover and drink nectar from the throat of this wonderful flower. Autumn evenings and Acidanthera were made for each other.

Allium: Amaryllidaceae

ે૨

A. CEPA PROLIFERUM GROUP—EGYPTIAN ONION · A. AFLATUNENSE ·
A. CHRISTOPHII—STARS OF PERSIA · A. GIGANTEUM · A. KARATAVIENSE ·
A. MOLY—LILY LEEK · A. URSINUM—RAMSONS, BUCK RAMS ·
A. TUBEROSUM—CHINESE CHIVE

illiam Robinson was unexpectedly curmudgeonly about alliums, writing in the mid-nineteenth century that they had little value in the garden, spread too much, and smelled when crushed. Vita Sackville-West replied to these accusations, writing: "For once I must disagree with that eminent authority. Some alliums have high value in the . . . garden; far from objecting to a desirable plant making a spreading nuisance . . . I am only too thankful that it should do so, and as for smelling nasty when crushed—well, who in his senses would wish to crush his own flowers?"

Today there is little debate over alliums, because most gardeners agree with the indomitable Vita's opinion. The various colors of ornamental alliums give them even greater allure. There are rosy purples, heavenly blues, daffodil yellows, subtle mauves and lilacs, and starry whites, and because alliums may keep their flowers for as long as a month, these colors make a valuable, lasting statement in the garden. The flowers are easily dried (just cut and hang upside-down in a dry spot) and therefore will continue on bravely in the house.

Alliums are pedigreed classic bulbs. The types that we associate with food have been cultivated since prehistoric times, and today their culinary popularity is reaching an all-time high. Allen Lacy calls the food alliums "blessed plants," and among those we grow are chives (*A. schoenoprasum*), leeks (*A. ampeloprasum* Porrum Group), onions (*A. cepa*), spring onions (*A. fistulosum*), shallots (*A. cepa* Aggregatum Group), and garlic (*A. sativum*, with its amusing synonym *A. controversum.*)

Author Abbie Zabar makes tiny bouquets with alliums from her rooftop garden of potted herbs.

Allen Paterson—director of the Royal Botanic Gardens in Ontario, former curator of the venerable Chelsea Physic Garden in London, and inventor of the word "alliophile"—points out that *all* alliums, even those we consider useful only as ornamentals, can be eaten, "though some flowers are charmingly perfumed . . . and to eat some would almost be akin to gobbling down lark's tongues."

All alliums are edible. These ornamental Chinese Chives (A. tuberosum) have been left to dry in the Fearrington Village herb garden, outside Pittsboro, North Carolina.

Abbie Zabar's alliums echo the shape of her lollipop topiaries. These alliums grow happily in pots, others are suited for almost any garden need.

The wacky appearance of the Egyptian Onion (A. Cepa, Proliferum Group) makes it a favorite with children.

Alliums, long associated with magic and medicine, grow in medieval gardens at the Cloisters, New York City.

Those lark's-tongues-type alliums make wonderful additions to perennial borders, rock gardens, and shuberies. So if alliums are so all-around exemplary, why did Robinson shun them? The answer lies in the fact that about 90 percent of the historical literature on this genus simply cannot get beyond the fact that pretty garden flowers and the much-maligned garlic are in the same genus. One old fogey wrote in 1930: "Alliums . . . would undoubtedly be much more popular if it were not for the fact that we associate this name with garlic and hence shun *all* members of the tribe."

Fortunately, the growing popularity of pesto and of Chicken Baked with Twenty Garlics has helped an earlier, more fastidious generation overcome the Fear of Offending. Now that the formerly plebeian garlic and onion are welcome in almost every kitchen, the way is clear for ornamental alliums to find their way into almost every garden.

The distinction between growing alliums for culinary uses and simply growing them as garden ornaments has always been a bit hazy. The ancient Celts must have eaten their alliums, because their word for "hot," *all*, gave the genus its name. The Elizabethans grew alliums strictly for ornamental purposes, and Gerard reported that he had nine varieties while Parkinson boasted fourteen. (John Gerard and John Parkinson were two Elizabethan garden writers whose works—Gerard's *Herbal* and *Catalogus* and Parkinson's *Paradisi*—contain lists of plants that, among other things, help establish the dates when plants were introduced to cultivation.)

Alliums were useful in witchcraft and magic, especially in the vampire department. This may stem from the genus's genuine antiseptic qualities. Modern clinical experimentation confirms this ancient reputation. Members of the Onion Family, especially garlic, have proven themselves aids to reducing fever, speeding digestion, dilating blood vessels, and easing bronchial secretions. In the old days many illnesses were believed to be caused by spells and miasmas, so the healing properties of the Onion Family were interpreted as magical, too.

The magic reputation clung, and as late as the nineteenth century, Sorceror's Garlick (*A. magicum*) was offered for sale. But in the 1885 edition of *The Dictionary of Gardening,* this species took on a new name and identity. Rechristened *A. nigrum,* it was listed among thirty other ornamental alliums suitable for pleasure gardens.

Early in this century, Louise Beebe Wilder professed adoration for the alliums and grew sixty to seventy species in her New York garden. She especially loved their adaptability and bragged that she "transplanted them successfully in all seasons, whether in or out of bloom." Closer to our own time, Elizabeth Lawrence, the indomitable doyenne of Southern horticulture, grew at least thirteen kinds of alliums to assure their continual presence in her North Carolina garden from late March through August.

It's up to you whether you use your alliums for magic, for cooking, or simply for their unusual beauty, but in the following annotated allium list, there are bound to be several classics suited to your tastes.

One of the oldest in cultivation, the Egyptian Onion (*A. cepa* Proliferum Group) certainly deserves the title

Allium giganteum *sways above the heads of Stars-of-Persia* (**A. christophii**) *at Wave Hill in New York.*

the Amusing Allium. Its thick hollow stem resembles an old gray-green rubber garden hose filled to the bursting point. This hose-stem rises to a flowerless top that sprouts a cluster of baby onions. Some of these baby onions wave about on further bits of garden hose. The whole thing looks like a pin-headed, green Hydra, and it's bound to capture the attention of any visitor to your ornamental herb garden. The Elizabethans, who loved oddities and curiosities, grew it in their flower gardens,

At the Whiteside–Hales
garden in Cold Spring,
New York, Tall Alliums
(here A. aflatunense)
add interest in early summer.

Allium karataviense *is
grown primarily for its
foliage rather than its
disappointing flowers.*

but it retired to kitchen gardens later in the eighteenth century. As late as the 1870s, the little groups of onions at the top were decapitated and sold at Covent Garden as a treat for pickling, but now this amusing plant seldom appears.

Allium neopolitanum of northern Italy came into cultivation in 1788, and because of its fine, sweet smell, it has always been the Socially Acceptable Allium. This is one of the very few tender species, but it will grow happily outside in zones 8, 9, and 10. Californians and other warm-climate gardeners should note that William Robinson wrote over a century ago that the lemon orchards of Provence were carpeted in the sweet white flowers of *A. neopolitanum.* Although Louise Beebe Wilder wrote that she occasionally overwintered this bulb in New York, gardeners in zones colder than 7 might want to follow the dictates of old-fashioned parlor gardening and force these perfumers for pleasant winter-blooming bouquets.

Three Tall Alliums for the late-spring, early-summer garden are *A. christophii* (Stars-of-Persia), *A. giganteum,* and *A. aflatunense* (this one really needs a nickname). Stars-of-Persia was introduced from Turkestan in 1901, and although it has been called the "winsome onion," since it stands two feet tall and its head may sometimes reach twelve inches in diameter, it might better be called the "awesome onion." Mrs. Wilder was wild for *A. christophii,* and Ms. Sackville-West grew its metallic purple majesty at Sissinghurst alongside bearded irises.

About the same height, but with smaller heads and a less formal appearance, *A. aflatunense* was brought from China and introduced by the famous Dutch bulb firm Van Tubergen in 1900. This allium makes excellent cut flowers, and the dried seed heads will stand for a long time in the garden. *A. giganteum* is a spectacular if somewhat familiar sight, an 1883 introduction from Central Asia. Because of its absolutely round head and its lofty height, this allium should be nicknamed Basketball Allium. It has bluish-lilac, perfectly globular flower heads on stalks that may tower as high as five feet. All of these Tall Alliums make nice dried flowers.

A. karataviense, on the other hand, is a Short Allium. It hunkers around six inches off the ground. Alliophile Wilder called it "a rather astonishing plant." Unlike other alliums, it is often grown more for its broad glaucous leaves than for its big muddy-white flower. Russian explorers first spotted this plant in the mountains of Central Asia, but it was not until 1876 that a Dr. Regel sent bulbs to his father in St. Petersburg. Its official debut was two years later, when it was introduced to the rest of the world.

Two smaller, broad-leafed alliums are the easiest to grow and are perfect for naturalizing in woodlands. *A. moly,* the Lily Leek or Golden Garlic, was one of Pliny's "most precious plants," and although it has an official introduction date in the seventeenth century, the Romans may have brought it from Spain and France into England. Peter Collinson, an expert on New World plants, sent these yellow alliums from his London garden to Philadelphian John Bartram during one of their many pre–Revolutionary War plant exchanges. Elizabeth Lawrence especially liked the name Lily Leek, "not that it looks or smells at all like a lily," she wrote, "but because I like those languishing William Morris names." Wilder notes that these are not wonderful in the rock garden, but Robinson channels their rampant behavior wonderfully by recommending that they be naturalized with wild flowers and ferns. At one time, *A. moly* was believed to be symbolic of prosperity if found in one's garden. Now that hard times are upon us, this prolific yellow wonder is certainly more attainable than a Porsche in the driveway.

Looking almost like a white version of *A. moly* is *A. ursinum*, Ramsons or Buck Rams. The leaves look like and often grow well in the same shady areas as Lily-of-the-valley, but really do have a strong onion scent. For this reason, keep them away from pathways or garden edges where constant bruising will undoubtedly occur. Their best use is on the edge of a woodland where, in springtime, their starry-white blossoms will peek out like groups of mischievous wood fairies.

One of the nicest alliums is sweetly scented *A. tuberosum*. This is a graceful white flower that stands about two feet tall on slender but strong scapes. Mrs. Wilder called this plant *A. odorum,* a former name, but old photographs show she was almost certainly referring to *A. tuberosum.* Besides the fact that this plant sends forth its perfume so freely, it is also most garden-worthy for its late blooming period. In the North it blooms in August; in warmer climates it flowers earlier. After its first bloom, one can either promptly remove the flower stalks to promote a possible second bloom in mid-autumn or leave the heads to dry slowly to a beautiful light brown dotted with prominent black seeds.

Nicholas Culpepper wrote one of the most popular and accessible herbals of the seventeenth century. If there are those still wary of the ornamental onion, take heed of his venerable advice: "Let it be taken inwardly with great moderation—outwardly you may make more bold with it."

*White starry-flowered Ramsons (**A. ursinum**) naturalized in an English woodland.*

Dried **Allium tuberosum**
and bittersweet berries make a
pretty Thanksgiving
door decoration at the
author's home.

Allium tuberosum,
or Chinese Chive, is a
sweetly scented flower for the
autumn garden at Wave Hill,
New York.

13

Anemone: Ranunculaceae

A. CORONARIA—FLORIST'S ANEMONE

It is sometimes said (and always with bitter countenance) that familiarity breeds contempt, but the common, everyday Florist's Anemone smiles in the face of this sour old saw. Centuries ago Parkinson wrote that anemones "are to be found almost in all places, with all persons," and today they remain unflaggingly popular, found all winter long at every street-corner florist. But no one seems to complain about Florist's Anemones: a bunch of these brightly colored beauties always seems as fresh and welcome as a child's handmade greeting card.

Anemones have been included in all the best gardens in history. The ancient Egyptians grew anemones and roses among their topiaries, and the cool, walled gardens of the Persians, which contained only choice plants, usually included a few bright anemone faces. Dioscorides and Pliny wrote about them, and anemones were considered indispensable in old monastery gardens even though, as members of the poisonous Ranunculus Family, they were of no medicinal use. The Tudors, including the famous flower fancier John Parkinson, loved them, they were found in early English cottage gardens, and they moved to the New World as soon as the first Europeans did.

Anemone coronaria— *pictured here along a hedge in Colonial Williamsburg, Virginia—has no use as food or medicine, yet was popular in the earliest American gardens.*

When the island of Manhattan had barely more than 1,000 Dutch inhabitants, most of them poor and hard-working, there were already small gardens sporting bulbs such as tulips, lilies, fritillaries, and anemones. An early visitor to New Amsterdam reported that by 1674 the English had taken over but the "Netherlander" flowers, such as the Florist's Anemone, remained. In those days the "finer bulbs" such as Anemones, Tuberoses, and Hyacinths were treated with elaborate care: cosseted in raised beds and dug up for seasonal storage,

*The Battenfeld family of Red Hook, New York, joins centuries of flower fanciers by specializing in Anemones. By the late 1600s, there were already three hundred varieties of **Anemone coronaria** being grown by florists.*

whether it was really necessary or not. By the time the Colonies became a free nation, Thomas Jefferson and family friend Lady Skipwith were growing double-flowered Anemones imported from France. (Lady Skipwith was the wife of Sir Peyton Skipwith and an enthusiastic gardener at Prestwould, their home on the Dan River in Virginia.)

The Anemone is not particularly easy to grow, it has no medicinal value, and it cannot be eaten. The only reason for its long-lasting popularity must be that everyone all along has found it just as pretty and charming as we do today. There is a shining, innocent beauty in Anemones that just makes one want to have them around. It is difficult to explain their draw, but it's sort of like sex appeal without the sex.

Anemone coronaria is native to Mediterranean regions and Central Asia. In the past, great drifts of the wild red, blue, and white flowers spread over the hills of the Holy Land, leading scholars to hypothesize that these are probably the flowers in "consider the lilies of the field, how they grow; they toil not, nor do they spin. . . ." (Even ancient writers made note of the guileless appeal of the anemone.) It is these same exposed hillsides that gave rise to the nickname "windflower" because, as Pliny wrote, "the flower hath the propertie to open when the wind doth blow." Another source for the name might be that the flower grows on windy, exposed hillsides.

Although wild hillsides of anemones would be found flaming with red, blue, and white, Florists's Anemones come in far more colors. Dick Battenfeld, owner of a three-generation commercial cut-flower operation in Red Hook, New York, notes that today's shine with "potent reds and purples . . . undiluted whites . . . deepest cobalt to bleached bone . . . reds that run the gamut from inky cabernet to fire engine neon, watercolor wash blues and heliotrope violets . . . carmine, salmon, ultramarine and sky . . . and half a dozen distinct pinks." Guileless, yes; boring, no.

There are two stories that are invariably associated with *Anemone coronaria,* both so widely repeated that they are bound to appear someday in a "Classic Comics" version. The first story would be entitled "The Bishop and the Miracle."

During the Crusades (eleventh, twelfth, and thirteenth centuries), Umberto, Bishop of Pisa, sailed off to the Holy Land to give his blessings to the troops stationed abroad. As is usually the way when high-rankers visit the enlisteds, Umberto sought the most possible political leverage from his trip, and to that end he ordered his sailing vessel to return to Italy loaded with soil from the Holy Land. This, he decided, would be spread on the cemetery attached to his cathedral so that those who died while fighting the infidels could be sent home to be interred in extra-holy ground. What happened next was a PR dream.

The soil that was spread on Campo Santo obviously contained Anemone tubers, because the next spring the cemetery bloomed with countless red flowers, "born of the blood of the martyrs." The bishop promptly proclaimed a miracle, and the expense and waste of the unsuccessful Crusades were therefore justified. Which may explain the presence of Anemones in all those old monastery gardens.

But Alice Coats, dauntless plant detective of our own century and author of the excellent *Flowers and Their Histories,* was skeptical. "So runs the tale; but it seems strange that Bishop Umberto should not have already been familiar with this anemone, which grows wild in Italy . . . and was a popular flower for garlands in the days of the Greeks and Romans," she wrote. (*Coronaria,* of course, means "garland.")

These bright flowers had been living quietly in Pisa for a long time, only to become celebrated when Umberto "discovered" them. Galen, a Greek physician and writer who lived in Rome during the second century A.D., had complained, years before the idea of a Crusade, that the herbalists of Rome knew the plants of Crete and the Orient but ignored those growing on the outskirts of their own city. As Rome went, Pisa probably did as well, and even today imported things seem "more special."

"The Covetous Burgomaster" is the name of the second "Classic Comics" story. In the early 1600s, the best-known grower of *A. coronaria* was a gardener in Paris named M. Bachelier. For ten years no one else could come near the glorious successes this Parisian had with anemones, but he point-blank refused to share any seeds with anybody. His selfishness became infamous, to the point where his undoing became an international plot.

The burgomaster, or mayor, of Antwerp made a request (that could not be refused) to visit M. Bachlier's

**Anemones in a shady
naturalized bulb garden in
Colonial Williamsburg,
Virginia.**

17

garden just at the time when the tiny, fuzzy Anemone seeds were ripe for harvesting. While swanning through the garden in his fur-trimmed civic robes, the burgomaster managed to drop said garment right on an Anemone bed. At this, his servant rushed over and picked up said furry robe and, as planned, all the hirsute seeds sticking to it. The servant beat a hasty retreat to the carriage with robe and seeds, and an early episode of *Mission Impossible* was in the can. The covetous burgomaster then distributed his stolen goods to friends all over Europe, not hesitating to brag about which truck they had fallen off the back of. The story spread so far and wide that for a long time progeny of the ill-gotten goods were jokingly called French Anemones.

Those French Anemones didn't stay put for long. In the seventeenth century, Huguenot and Flemish refugees were forced to flee religious intolerance in their own countries and resettle in Protestant England. These people—mostly middle-class merchants or artisans involved in weaving, embroidery, and lacemaking—were industrious and hardworking, and brought to their new homes a "hobby" that changed forever the way we look at and think about flowers. These people and their fellow countrymen back in France gradually became known as florists.

In those days a florist was a specialist in a particular flower, not someone who ran a flower shop. The first florists were flower breeders intent upon creating absolutely perfect flowers. *Anemone coronaria* was among the very first florist flowers. John Rea wrote his book *Flora* in 1665, giving instructions for "all requisites belonging to a florist." For at least the next century *Anemone coronaria* remained the most popular object of the florist's desire. Feasts, societies, shows, and lots of socializing went along with floristry, and at the beginning of the nineteenth century there were a total of eight accepted florists' flowers: Carnation, Pink, Auricula, Polyanthuse, Anemone, Hyacinth, and Tulip. These were joined later by the Pansy and Dahlia. Since there were so few florists' flowers, each got a great deal of attention, which resulted in zillions of crosses and varieties. By Rea's time, there were already 300 varieties of *Anemone coronaria*.

Early scientists found the florists ridiculous. Linnaeus, the eighteenth-century botanist who invented the plant naming system we still use today, was wary of them: "These men cultivate a science peculiar to themselves, the mysteries of which are only known to the adepts; nor can such knowledge be worth the attention of the botanist; wherefore let no botanist ever enter their Societies."

But botanist's boycott or not, floristry eventually died out as a result of modern times. When the Industrial Revolution came along, the weaver-florists and artisan-florists were forced to leave their cottage industries and their rural cottages for work in urban factories. The factories—and all the houses for people who worked in them—began to encroach upon the land where flowers once grew. Spare time for flower breeding disappeared into seventy-two-hour work weeks, and, inevitably, the passion for floristry faded and many once-cosseted flowers disappeared forever.

Today we no longer have 300 varieties of *Anemone coronaria* to choose from. Two principal strains remain, however: 'De Caen' and 'St. Brigid'. Although there is some disagreement among the ranks, most agree that both strains are children of the ancient *A. coronaria*. Certainly both are wonderful enough to have in the garden and in the house.

Other anemones to try in your bulb garden include *A. blanda,* a tuber from southeastern Europe and Asia Minor introduced in 1898. This flower was a favorite of Elizabeth Lawrence's, who labeled it "one of the best little bulbs." Lawrence also planted *A. apennina* to carry on after her Blandas finished. But the Coronarias are the anemones pictured here.

Although Pliny said that anemones bloom when the wind blows, the winds whispering through the native lands of these flowers are warm Mediterranean breezes—they do not last long in colder weather. Bulb lover E. A. Bowles wrote that "their cultivation must be pursued on the buy-and-die system. . . . I occasionally invest in a hundred or so to get at least one season's fun out of them." And so should you.

Actually, gardeners in the warmer areas of the South and, probably, many in the Pacific Northwest can leave

The ferny foliage of Anemones looks pretty against the straplike leaves of Bluebells.

their Florist's Anemones in the ground all the time. When the ground outside thaws and warms, soak the tubers for eighteen hours to make them swell slightly. After planting, fresh green leaves should appear in sixteen to twenty days.

Tubers planted in April will produce summer blooms, and those planted out in June will add festive colors to autumn. *Anemone coronaria* does just fine in the shade but needs humus-rich soil. The plants need lots of water; a lack of it at any time will cause bloom failure. Under commercial conditions, a single crown can produce up to twenty-five blooms in one season.

Anemones have had such prolonged popularity and such legions of ardent devotees that it is odd the Victorian language of flowers should assign negative meanings to them. At one time they meant "sickness" or "forlornness"; a cheery-looking bouquet of anemones delivered to your Victorian-era sweetie let her know under no uncertain terms "you are forsaken." What a shame to make such a nice flower do the dirty work.

Forget the Victorians and remember Parkinson instead: "The anemones . . . are so pleasant and so delightsome flowers that the sight of them doth enforce an earnest longing desire in the mind of anyone to be in possession of some of them at the least. . . . " Yes, indeedy, sex appeal without the sex.

Begonia: Begoniaceae

B. GRANDIS—HARDY BEGONIA

There are many gardeners who swore they would never grow a gladiolus—until they fell for the old-fashioned, graceful wands of *G. byzantinus*. There are also many who turned up their noses at all chrysanthemums—until they were charmed by the scented leaves and creamy shirt-button flowers of Feverfew *(C. parthenium)*. And gardeners who have eschewed all begonias as troublesome and not worth the effort might be surprised to learn that the genus has a fascinating history and offers a shyly beautiful, hardy species that deserves a place in just about any autumn perennial garden.

Many turn up their noses at begonias because they simply do not know enough about them. Although some experts acknowledge as few as 350 *Begonia* species, *Hortus Third* and other authorities report that over 1,000 species and more than 10,000 hybrids and cultivars have been recorded. Those ubiquitous begonia "bedders" that bear much responsibility for the "bedding-out" craze in the mid-nineteenth century, are most emphatically *not* the only ones. Begonias offer great variety in the shape, size, and color of their foliage and, besides the standard mounded begonia habit, there are ground-covering creepers and types that tower up to ten feet tall. Some begonias have enjoyed unwavering popularity as houseplants for more than a century, and at least one begonia is hardy outdoors as far north as New York City. The American Begonia Society, through its voice *The Begonian,* would be the first to say that lack of appreciation for begonias is really just lack of education.

Many flower lovers may be astonished that the begonia was not invented in the 1950s. Although there is some confusion about the initial introduction, it's most likely that Charles Plumier (1646–1706), a French botanist who traveled widely in tropical America, discovered the first species in Santo Domingo around 1690. He named his new plant *Begonia* to immortalize fellow countryman Michel Begon—his patron and, at one time, French governor of Santo Domingo.

Although begonias were first introduced more than three hundred years ago, they actually spent more than a century languishing on the "what shall we do with this" shelf until James Veitch took this little exile into his able hands. Born in Exeter, Devon, in 1792, he was the son of a gardener from Scotland (at that time the wealthy who sought status would hire only Scottish gardeners). In 1835 young Veitch opened a small nursery in Devon's prosperous market town just in time to capitalize on the Victorian fad for tender hothouse plants. Veitch was a sponsor of plant exploration (including "Chinese" Wilson's discovery of the Regal Lily) and of hybridization, especially of begonias, and by

Begonia grandis is the hardy boy of the genus, overwintering sixty miles north of New York City. This mound was photographed at Montrose Nursery, Hillsborough, North Carolina, in October.

Tropical begonias in the Tavares family garden in the Dominican Republic.

*The red stems of **Begonia grandis** glow in the autumn sunshine at Wave Hill.*

1853 his innovative firm moved to King's Road, Chelsea. More exploration and many crosses later, Veitch and his begonias achieved wild success.

New introductions from South America gave rise to clever hybridizing, and by the mid-nineteenth century, begonias—along with salvias, geraniums, and other "stove" or hothouse plants—helped sweep away all that Capability Brown (1716–83) and the "landskip" movement had tried to achieve. Richardson Wright wrote in 1934: "People, wearied of the flowerless gardens of the landscapists, began to take their flowers neat. . . ." The unfortunate result of all their deprivation—known variously as carpet bedding, bedding out, or mosaiculture—seems risable today. Begonias, caladiums, cannas, and other tropicals were grown by the thousands in private hothouses, only to have a very short life planted outside in the garden. As soon as their peak of bloom was slightly past, they were ripped up and replaced with the next tidal wave of flowers. Victorians would not hesitate to tear out every single plant in their intricately patterned gardens several times each season! The waste, let alone the work, seems unthinkable today. But, before modern gardeners jump to deride this style of gardening (and all begonias along with it), remember that today's more personal, romantic style of gardening was, like carpet bedding, a popular garden style in the past. Although it might seem impossible that mosaiculture could ever become a fad again, remember that there are countless women over thirty-five who swore they would never again wear a miniskirt. Fashion is fashion is fashion.

Another Victorian garden style begonias helped popularize was parlor gardening. While many of us still grow houseplants, few have the ornately designed glass cases, ferneries, fountains, plant stands, and bulb tables essential to the grand scale of parlor gardening executed by our great-grandmothers. In a delightfully illustrated Victorian book, *Window Gardening* (1873), author Henry Williams states that "it is unequaled . . . as a showy plant for picturesque ornament in the room or conservatory."

Thus, the begonia does figure importantly in our great horticultural past, and for those still reluctant to embrace bedding out and for those who don't garden indoors, there is an old-fashioned, hardy, perennial begonia that deserves a quiet corner in modern gardens almost everywhere.

Begonia grandis, also known as Hardy Begonia, makes

a two-foot-high mound of crisp, sparkling leaves that ably support cascades of pink blossoms. The red flower stems branch in a most graceful manner, and their striking color is echoed in reddish markings on each leaf. Flowers and leaves each have a kind of luminosity, as if filled with a liquid suspension of softly reflective glitter. If an elf took a crunchy bite from *B. grandis*, cartoonlike stars would fly from his lips.

Begonias are monoecious—that is, they have separate male and female flowers on the same plant. Although the male flowers are considered "more showy," many prefer the prominent wings of the female. But what makes *B. grandis* really special is that this native of China and Japan begins to bloom prolifically in late summer, keeps up the pace all throughout autumn, and then, with the first killing frost, merely retreats under the cold ground until new leaves poke through the following May. It will definitely overwinter in zone 6 and may make it through zone 5. This is the thrifty Yankee's begonia.

Two sources give dates of introduction as early as 1804 or as late as 1939, but most credit 1812, when it was featured in Curtis's *Botanical Magazine,* as the correct year. Although formerly known as *B. evansiana* (the plant explorer Thomas Evans of the East India Company brought the plant to England) or *B. discolor* ("of two or different colors"), *B. grandis* ("large, showy") is the accepted if somewhat misleading (because it is not the largest) name of choice today.

Begonia grandis is quite happy in a shady position, but will take a lot of sun in a northern garden. Elizabeth Lawrence planted her colchicums where their mauve autumn flowers would be enhanced with the "hermosa pink of the hardy begonia," still in full bloom. The red stems also look nice when glowing near the red stems of *Oenothera missourensis,* which blooms earlier in the season. Allen Lacy, the modern connoisseur of the fall garden, wrote: "If placed where it catches the last low rays of the sun from behind, *Begonia grandis* offers a sight that is one of the epiphanies of autumn."

Tender begonias were (and still are) an essential element in the extravagant practice of bedding-out or mosaiculture. Reviled by many modern gardeners, bedding-out should be considered in its historical context, such as here at Versailles.

Caladium: Araceae

❧

The Three Cs—caladiums, cannas, and colocasias—belong to the Never-Say-Never group of plants. Having long banned these to the "tasteless oasis" zone, many Northerners have enjoyed sudden conversions when they see how beautifully these bold plants are utilized in the tropics. The good news is that because all three are either tubers or rhizomes that may be dug up and stored inside during cold weather, caladiums, cannas, and colocasias can also flourish in more northern gardens. There they may serve as reminders that there are probably no downright vulgar plants, but instead, plants that suffer from bad associations.

Like begonias, the Three Cs have a bad reputation arising from their longtime association with bedding-out. Bedding-out or carpet gardening, had a formidable opponent in William Robinson, born in 1838 and died only three years shy of his centenary, a gardener and tremendously influential author whose books are still constantly reprinted. Anyone who has read *The English Flower Garden* will know that Robinson *hated* bedding out. "Marshalling the flowers in stiff lines and geometric patterns," he wrote, "is entirely a thing of our own precious time, and carpet gardening is simply a further remove in ugliness." He held this style of gardening responsible for "the ugliest and most formally set out and planted gardens ever made in England."

Okay, okay! But Robinson's dislike for bedding-out may have had its roots in his past. As a young gardener, he worked in Ireland on the estate of Sir Hunt Johnson-Walsh. There he was responsible for huge expanses of

**Caladium *x* hortulanum
'White Christmas'
sparkles at the
Brooklyn Botanic Garden.**

greenhouses. One winter night, while Robinson had an evening out, the fires also went out. Every single tender plant in the valuable Johnson-Walsh collection was reduced to soggy black jelly. Although this disgrace was only a momentary setback in Robinson's distinguished career, ever afterward he despised greenhouses, even to the extent of refusing, fifty years later, to have them at his own house and garden at Gravetye.

On this side of the Atlantic, Louise Beebe Wilder, who was born forty years after Robinson but whose professional life overlapped with his very long one, took a more practical stance on the bedding-out controversy: "It requires some fortitude in this day to express approval of the bedding-out system. It has departed, or should have, with the days of antimacassars and hand-painted tambourines, and no one wants this period of terrible and useless ornament to return; yet it seems to me that there are times and places where we may still bed out with propriety and even grace."

Wilder hit the positioning problem right on the head when she wrote that bedding-out was especially useful "where there are flower beds on a terrace that extends along the facade of the dwelling. . . . Such a conspicuous situation should not be at the mercy of the ups and downs, the defections, and general uncertainness that prevails in the region devoted to perennials and annuals, where their half-wild ways are simply an additional charm." It is this area, the "betweenity—neither house nor garden," that calls for the "persistent color and exact arrangement only to be attained by the use of law-abiding bedders. . . ." It is this betweenity that the

27

American gardener Louise Beebe Wilder deemed caladiums essential for the "betweenity" linking house and garden. This tropical native thrives in the patio garden of the Tavares family in the Dominican Republic.

tropical gardener calls the veranda, the patio, or the terrace, and it is here that tropical plants like caladiums can solve a design dilemma for almost any gardener.

Caladium is a genus of about fifteen tuberous perennials native to tropical America. Introduced to Europe two centuries ago, caladiums were first confined to hothouses, then became popular Victorian houseplants, and now are frequently seen outside in warm weather gardens. *Caladium* has many aliases. Some call them Elephant's Ear, a too frequently used nickname better deserved by *Colocasia;* or Mother-in-law-plant, also better claimed by *Dieffenbachia;* or Angel-wings, which is, a common type of *Begonia.* Caladium is easy. Why not call it that?

The derivation of the name is a little confused, with some pulling up *kaladion,* "cup," and others *kelady,* "unknown"—a South American Indian word. The date of introduction is also somewhat controversial, but most sources agree that Portuguese sailors first took *C.*

bicolor to Madeira in 1773. A horticultural variety of *C. bicolor,* var. *poecile,* is called Wild Taro in the West Indies, where it is boiled and eaten like potatoes. (This further confuses this genus with *Colocasia,* the true Taro, which is a major tropical food crop.) Although a lazy gardener might be tempted to eat his caladium tubers rather than store them for the winter, he must be sure to follow recipes carefully. But be forewarned: Caladiums are a natural emetic or purge, and when prepared incorrectly, can cause severe distress—a fact that should curb any caladium cravings by the curious.

The most popular caladiums are *C.* × *hortulanum,* the Fancy-leaved Caladiums of mixed hybrid origin. Those with heart-shaped leaves show the influence of *C. bicolor,* while those with lanceolate, strap-shaped leaves reveal genes inherited from *C. picturatum,* a Peruvian introduction made in the 1850s.

Fancy-leaved Caladiums have unfancy flowers. In fact, their flowers are rarely seen, a characteristic that made them very popular with Victorian parlor gardeners. Having gotten off on the wrong foot by initially trying and failing to raise roses and primulas indoors, the Victorians turned to more sensible and easier-to-raise foliage plants. Tovah Martin records: "Flowerless plants were 'chaste'—an attribute most decidedly to their credit in Victorian eyes." Those who have giggled at other *Araceae* flowers like anthuriums or arums know that the aroids have the plant world's most embarrassing flowers. It's just as well that their cousin caladium rarely sports its grayish-yellow flower spike.

The red, pink, white, cream, or green markings of Fancy-leaved Caladiums are just the thing for a shady spot. Their large leaves have a delicate, slightly draping quality, so a pretty grouping looks like cotton-lawn hankies drying over a small shrub. Leaves with iridescent white markings bring snowy coolness to hot summer, green ones with tiny red and white spots remind one of Christmas confetti, and matte reddish-pink leaves can enliven an otherwise dull period amongst the shrubbery. Although Caladiums can be used anywhere, somehow they seem to look best on a terrace, in a gazebo, or right next to the house. The Victorians called tropical plants "the wild beasts of horticulture," but Caladiums just love domestic life.

Caladiums become very unhappy when the temperature falls below 55 degrees; except in Hawaii, it is risky to overwinter them in the United States. In the Deep South, plant out the tubers at the same same time as Gloriosa Lily, Society Garlic, and Agapanthus. Farther north, start the tubers inside at 70 to 80 degrees and harden off by putting them outside—in a sheltered shady spot—for a little time each day. Gradually increase the outside period, aiming at planting out around mid-June or two weeks after the date for setting out tomato plants in your area. Plenty of water is essential, but so is perfect drainage. Before the first frost, the tubers must be dug and cleaned. It is easiest to store them in an onion bag or an old stocking, but remember the old saying, "Stay alive at 55" and keep them in a warm place.

Caladiums will fade if they get too much sun and will rip if they get too much breeze. Take a tip and grow them as do gardeners in Bali and the Dominican Republic—tuck them in peaceful niches in the "betweenity," and, for fun, try to find the perfect color and leaf pattern for your position, avoid "marshalling . . . in stiff lines and geometric patterns" and you may even please a diehard Robinsonian. Frances Perry recorded that an American named H. Nehrling once collected 1,500 named Caladium cultivars, so there is a long way to go before quitting on Caladiums. Never say never.

Caladiums are the perfect solution for a difficult shady spot, whether in tropical areas or in colder climates.

Canna: Cannaceae

C. INDICA—INDIAN SHOT · C. × GENERALIS—COMMON GARDEN CANNA

Cannas are second in the Never-Say-Never series of plants. These tall, brightly flowered and big-leaved rhizomatous perennials can bring back especially painful memories for Southerners who only picture cannas growing in the center of whitewashed, inside-out, discarded automobile tires. Every region of the country has its own brand of bad taste, so all you Rebels should take this unattractive little piece of "Dixie-Trix," file it next to the custom of putting white sugar on white rice, and get on with life. Cannas can be a bright spot of hope for the late-summer and early-autumn garden, and just about everyone, not only Southerners, can take up the challenge of using these tropical plants well.

Cannaceae has only one genus, *Canna,* which claims about sixty species native to the tropics and subtropics. Although some cannas have economic value, most are cultivated today as ornamentals, and almost all in gardens are hybrid forms with complicated lineage.

Because the canna has been around so long, it is fairly prevalent in old garden books. There "Canna" is often placed alphabetically next to "Cannabis," an intriguing antique plant grown for its fancy foliage. William Robinson's *English Flower Garden* has a detailed engraving of this now-outlawed annual, which he liked because it was "one of few plants that thrive in small London gardens." Both plants derive their names from the Celtic *can* or "reed."

Cannas were introduced to English and European gardens from the American tropics more than 400 years ago. They were soon distributed widely, as people all over the world discovered practical ways to use them. Spanish missionaries in the early colonies used their hard, round seeds as rosary beads, and in other tropical regions they were made into prayer beads for Buddhist and Islamic devotions. Today in Hawaii they are still strung in ornamental leis and inserted into dried gourds to make rattles called *'uli 'uli* needed in executing special hula dances.

The earliest *Canna* species introduced, *C. indica,* hit the Old World in 1570 from Central and South America and the West Indies. It was called Indian Shot, because its seeds were hard enough to replace ordinary lead shot from guns. This species grows four to six feet tall and, having escaped from cultivation long before there were old tires, has naturalized throughout the Deep South.

Other parts of the plant found use in native baby nurseries. The Tunebos Indians of Colombia and Ecuador wrapped newborns in large canna leaves, and *C. edulis* yields the Queensland arrowroot used in biscuits eaten by the little nippers when they are a bit past the swaddling stage. This edible canna was introduced from Peru in 1820 and is now an important food crop in Australia.

Cannas were introduced to Europe (as indoor plants) from the New World in 1570, but did not move into the garden until the mid-1800s. Here the modern hybrid 'Longwood Yellow' in a traditional conservatory setting at Longwood Gardens, Kennett Square, Pennsylvania.

Even when relegated to the background, variegated-leaf cannas stand out in Edith Eddelman's Durham, North Carolina, fall garden.

The canna has long held court in Southern gardens. This eight-foot-tall garden hybrid 'Pretoria' was photographed in October at Montrose Nursery, Hillsborough, North Carolina.

Venerable garden designers such as William Robinson, Vita Sackville-West, and Russell Page found the canna an appealing autumn addition. Here, 'City of Portland' hybrid in the late-summer border at the Brooklyn Botanic Garden.

For years cannas were used in Europe only as hothouse plants. The first attempts at utilizing them as bedding plants (in other words, taking them out of hothouses into the real garden world—even if only for a few months) occurred sometime around 1846. That's when a French consular agent posted in South America, Monsieur Année, brought cannas back to his garden in Paris. Their showiness caused an immediate sensation, and Année started creating his own hybrids.

Venerable species that helped weave the entangled web of Canna Family trees were *C. warscewiczii* (1849) for variegated leaf genes; *C. flaccida* (1788), which contributed large flower size to *C. × orchiodes,* the Orchid-flowered Canna bred in 1893; and *C. × generalis,* the Common Garden Canna group that includes what are now called "Crozy" (Crozet) or French Cannas.

Monsieur Crozet of Lyon (who would undoubtedly roll in his grave to see his name spelled "Crozy") worked on double-flowered hybrids, and by 1874, Shirley Hibberd gleefully recorded their existence in *The Floral World and Garden Guide.* The canna rage spread to England and America, and in 1907, the Royal Horticultural Society's garden at Wisely tested more than 200 varieties of cannas, selecting fifty from that number for Awards of Merit.

Cannas have scarlet, apricot, orange, pinkish, or yellow flowers that may rise as tall as twelve feet. The decorative leaves, described beautifully in *Hortus Third* as "large, simple, entire," have an elemental beauty sometimes missing in other fancy-leaved plants. A single plant has a good number of leaves, and canna foliage may come in many different colors, from purplish brown to lime green. Between lots of flowers and lots of leaves, sometimes it seems almost impossible that so much plant could come from one rhizome.

Cannas thrive in midsummer heat but must have lots of water. Their cultivation is similar to that of the other two Cs (caladiums and colocasias): in all areas except the very warmest, they must be planted out and dug up between frosts.

There are very few difficulties in growing Common Garden Cannas, but there have indeed been problems with placement. In 1913, Neltje Blanchan grappled boldly with the Never-Say-Never series in *The American Flower Garden:* "What shall be done with cannas? They give bold, brilliant color effects which are at once their glory and the despair of anyone who tries to reconcile the tropical-looking plants to the vegetation of a northern garden. Certainly they shall not be placed in a circular bed, with or without elephant's ears [colocasia or caladium] that so frequently accompany them."

Well, certainly not. Other garden movers and shakers have experimented with this exuberant plant. William Robinson, champion of old-fashioned flowers, found canna's "grace" especially appealing, as well as its ability to withstand "the storms of autumn." Vita Sackville-West followed his advice and added cannas to her late-summer borders at Sissinghurst. English garden designer Russell Page created a water garden in Grasse in the south of France with a lush abundance of bankside agapanthuses, clivias, hostas, and cannas merging with the foliage of the water plants. Discussing cultivation on a smaller scale, Page wrote that "I like pot gardening and would use plants in pots on steps, low walls, and on my paved terrace, grouping them in simple flower pots of all sizes. I should use cannas, yuccas, and hedychium." In our own time, Linda Yang recommends that the city gardener use cannas as "quick fillers" while waiting for newly planted trees and shrubs to mature. She rightly points out that city gardeners have so little space that "toothless gaps" are particularly disheartening. Finally, Allen Lacy, who is quoted so many times because he is so downright quotable, describes a use for cannas that is probably not practical for many people: "In one of the most beautiful gardens I know, the bulb garden high on the slopes of Montjuich in Barcelona, rivers of thousands of pale pink cannas flow down through the landscape, a glorious sight in the lambent golden light of a late afternoon in October. Even true canna-haters—and there are some—would be converted as instantly as St. Paul on the road to Damascus."

Forget about old tires and consider the possibilities.

Chasmanthe: Iridaceae

C. AETHIOPICA—FLAME FLOWER

Stately chasmanthe is perfect for the house-plant hedonist. These four-foot-tall natives of the Cape of Good Hope flower in the dreariest part of winter without the aid of greenhouse or cold treatment. Chasmanthes require no special attention, aren't bothered by pests or diseases, yet they are nothing short of spectacular—no-pain-but-plenty-of-gain plants for everyone.

No one has ever accused Thomas Jefferson of being a hedonist, but scholars know that he ordered *Chasmanthe aethiopica* for his cool greenhouse at Monticello. Present Monticello greenhouse manager Peggy Newcomb makes sure that this floral tradition is carried on, each year filling the conservatory with the bright orange-red flowers of *C. aethiopica* and the yellow flowers of *C. floribunda*. There are greenhouses and conservatories on Jefferson's mountaintop, but you can re-create this outstanding eighteenth-century tribute to floral exoticism using nothing more than a big pot, some soil, and a sunny window.

Despite the tremendous plant they produce, chasmanthe corms are scarcely larger than those of crocuses. They are available in late summer and autumn and should be planted in your large pot as soon as they arrive. Place the corms about two inches deep in sandy soil, and, although some sources advise otherwise, Newcomb says she gets the best results when she uses a lot of corms "all packed together" in one deep pot. (The depth is necessary because chasmanthes make a lot of roots.) Keep the pot absolutely dry until you see a few green leaves popping up. At this point start to water the plant and continue to keep the soil moist, but not soggy, throughout the winter and spring. Put the pot in a sunny window, give it some room, and wait. *Chasmanthe* isn't called vigorous for nothing.

Over the next month or two, watch in wonder as leaf after leaf emerges from those small corms. Each one you buried will produce up to ten stiff, swordlike leaves, and, about January, tall flowering stalks will also appear. This is when life gets really exciting, because the flowers grow even taller than the leaves, sometimes surpassing four feet. With their bright color, prominent stamens, and curved and hooded shape, these flowers look like something you would pay a fortune for. (It's up to you whether you tell anyone they cost about the same as an ice-cream cone.)

Flowers will continue to open from the gracefully curved stalk for about a month. Then your chasmanthe will begin to die down, and once the leaves start to dry up, you can put them away for their beauty rest. Cut off the old foliage and keep the pots bone-dry. Newcomb turns Monticello's pots on their sides—soil, corms, and all—to make sure that they don't get watered accidentally, and gives them an out-of-the-way spot to carry on with their summer dormant period. Chasmanthes require absolutely nothing at this point and you may safely ignore them entirely.

Then, sometime in late autumn or early winter, peer into those sideways pots to see if *Chasmanthe* is beginning to stir. When new green leaves start to appear,

Peggy Newcomb forces huge yellow and red chasmanthes for the conservatory at Monticello. Pots of Chinese Sacred Lily sit underneath the spectacular foliage.

place the pots upright and give them a good watering. The foliage and flowering cycle will begin again. Then stand back and enjoy as, after months of total neglect, *Chasmanthe* shakes its feathers phoenixlike and gets on with the business of something-for-nothing.

Colchicum: Liliaceae

❧

*I*f not for their hardiness, beauty, and timing, colchicums should absolutely, positively be grown for their amusing nicknames. When guiding your boring old Uncle Kendell around the garden (an activity he always requests, if only to criticize your design, plant material, garden bench, or whatever), point out the colchicums and mention only their misleading nickname autumn crocus. But when your darling favorite Aunt Mary—who can barely walk but still is the sweetest and funniest person alive—wants a tour of "your wonderful garden," tell her she has to see the Nudist Colony you have planted. It will be a warm, golden autumn afternoon, so you will have set up tea on a table positioned near the colchicums, which will give off their pretty lilac glow as the sun gets low. Tell Aunt Mary you call this the Nudist Colony because those wonderful flowering bulbs are variously known as Naked Boys, Star-naked Boys, and Naked Nannies. This is just the sort of thing to bring a mischievous twinkle back to her eyes, and she'll love you for remembering that old ladies were once risqué young girls. If she's in the mood and you are lucky, your tea in the Nudist Colony will be the setting of some delightfully improper reminiscing.

The native habitat of colchicums is widespread, from the eastern Mediterranean to Turkestan, as well as in Europe and Britain. The proper name arises from Colchis, an ancient country south of the Caucasus Mountains on the Black Sea that is now the western part of the Soviet Republic of Georgia.

There's nothing better to liven up an autumnal landscape than a hillside of Naked Boys (Colchicum sp.)—seen here at Winterthur, former home of Henry Francis du Pont.

Colchicums, here photographed at the Cloisters in New York City, yield the powerful chemical colchicine, used medicinally since early Roman times.

Colchicums have been collected and written about for millennia. An old legend says that Medea was mixing a rejuvenating potion for her father-in-law, Eason, and when she spilled a few drops on the ground, up sprang colchicums. Although this bulb has long been known as the source of the powerful chemical colchicine, this is the only instance of its being associated with restoring youth.

Theophrastus (c. 371–287 B.C.), who was a friend and pupil of Plato and Aristotle, recognized colchicine as a poison and called it Ephemeron. This name is from the Greek *ephemeros,* "lasting one day," and some interpreted this to mean that the poison would kill in one day. But Theophrastus wrote that slaves would often eat colchicine to make themselves ill, not dead, and that the antidote (he doesn't say what) was readily available for self-cures. Still, the whole practice of eating colchicine as a way to escape work seems desparately suicidal. In the first century A.D., Dioscorides, in *De Materia Medica* (which remained an authoritative medical text for the next 1,400 years), further detailed colchicums and their dangerous properties. William Turner (c. 1508–68), who is regarded as the Father of British Botany, kept the first known records of native British plants and wrote that the poison would "strangle a man and kill him in the space of one day, even as some kind of toadstools do." Most Europeans were wary of the drug, but James I (1566–1625), it seems, did use colchicine, mixed with a powder ground from unburied skulls, in a cure for gout that has not survived to the present day.

Nowadays colchicine is used in homeopathic medicine: to restore vision after long hours of reading, to cure spots before the eyes, and to soothe certain kinds of skin eruptions. In the 1950s it became useful in human genetic study because it makes human cells easier to study under a microscope, and more recent research with colchicine involves seeking treatments for multiple sclerosis.

Whatever its uses, modern or ancient, colchicine is a powerful product, and it stands to reason that one would not dare to munch one's colchicum corms. The corms do, apparently, have a pleasant taste, and perhaps this is why the French have called them *mort-au-chien.* As the leaves and seeds also contain colchicine, it is probably a good idea after tidying up the colchicum bed, *not* to feed the foliage to pet rabbits or chickens, lest the result be *mort-au-lapin* or *mort-au-poulet.*

Although the plants have been around for ages, *Colchicum* is one of those complicated genera that lead otherwise authoritative botanists and horticulturists into abject despair over proper nomenclature.

There are between fifty and sixty species of *Colchicum,* which are divided into three main groups: autumn-flowering species; late-winter- and early-spring-flowering species; and tesselated species. The first is the group described here and has been popular in gardens since the 1600s. Clusius, an early bulb devotee (who liked colchicum but reserved his love for tulips), first described *Colchicum autumnale* 'Album' in 1601. In *Rariorum Plantarum Historia* he mentions that the bulb was found wild near Bristol in Avon. Parkinson enjoyed growing colchicums and described the nineteen he had, hinting at the confusion over names: "Some have also called them 'Filius ante Patrem,' Son Before the Father, because (as they think) it gives seed before flower." *Colchicum* seed heads do come in spring, the result of the previous autumn's pollination of flowers, and are then followed by the new batch of flowers later in fall—a reversal of the expected order, though not a reversal of the laws of botany.

For the stark raving amateur, just being able to distinguish an autumn-flowering colchicum from an autumn-flowering crocus is an achievement in itself. Although the flowers at first glance appear quite similiar, they are, in fact, not even in the same family. Colchicums are *Liliaceae,* crocuses are *Iridaceae.* The colchicum flower appears on a long perianth tube instead of a stalk, and, in the Lily Family, the ovary is superior. (This means that it is inside the perianth tube.) In crocuses, there is a very short scape and the ovary is below the perianth. A colchicum blossom has three separate styles (tubes between the ovary and the stigma which receive the pollen grains), while a crocus blossom has one style divided into three parts. To figure out any of these characteristics, you must carefully bisect the flower with a sharp scalpel. But if the flowers belong to someone who doesn't want you to cut them up, the third and easiest way to distinguish a colchicum from a crocus is that the former has six stamens and the latter only three.

It's a good thing that it is far more simple to grow these bulbs than it is to guess which one is which. E. A. Bowles, a colchicum lover and an expert on the genus,

Even colchicum expert E. A. Bowles found the nomenclature of this genus complicated. Most gardeners today call their garden variety colchicums "probably **autumnale,** *but maybe* **speciosum."** *This "probably" form was grown at the Cloisters.*

Nasturtiums help solve the 'bare-earth issue'' associated with planting large colchicum corms at the Brooklyn Botanic Garden.

was the first to admit how problematic identifying them can be. In *A Handbook of Crocus and Colchicums* he wrote: "For the botanist their evil ways are numerous indeed. . . . There can scarcely be a genus of plants that is harder to describe and classify."

There is nothing worse than an acquaintance who constantly refers to people one has never met, and as Bowles is frequently quoted in this book, it is only proper that Edward Augustus Bowles be introduced at this point.

He was born in 1865 at Myddleton House, near Enfield, in Middlesex, about ten miles outside of London. His father was Henry Carington B. Bowles, a colleague of Canon Ellacombe, one of the great Victorian vicar-gardeners, who created the famous garden at Bitton. (William Robinson loved the garden at Bitton and thought it one of the best of its times in Britain.) Young Bowles visited Bitton regularly, and Ellacombe became his mentor, giving him plants and recommending books that would offer practical information on the subject of garden-making. By the time Ellacombe died in 1916 at age ninety-two, Bowles had become a well-respected gardener, and writer, and the friend of plant explorer Reginald Farrer.

Many of the exotic plants in the Myddleton garden came from Farrer, and the two occasionally went exploring together. Farrer, whose passion for alpine plants is credited with defining the art of rock gardening for the twentieth century, was nicknamed "the Moraine Magician." Together he and Bowles created a rock garden at Myddleton that was considered the masterstroke of the entire property.

Bowles wrote many books before his death in 1954, and with various reprints appearing each year, his lively work remains accessible to readers today. Of his own garden he lamented that "many find the garden too museum-y to please them," but any gardener who devotes space to weirdly formed plants and calls it the Lunatic Asylum can't be all that uptight.

Read Bowles whenever you have a chance, and once you become acquainted with his words, you'll find you repeat them often, too. If you become really fond of him, you could do him no greater honor than to plant a nice collection of colchicums. Although he came from a slightly more straitlaced time, the gardener of a Lunatic Asylum could not help but be amused by the planter of a Nudist Colony.

As a general rule, colchicums appear in catalogues mailed in late spring, and then they will probably be shipped to you for an August planting. They are a bit awkward the first year because their corms are surprisingly large and it takes some skill to tuck them in among other plants. Try not to leave too much bare soil around them. Autumn rains will send mud splashing onto the delicate blooms and will mess up the effect of the lovely flower. Yellow nasturtiums look very pretty with colchicums, and because many leaves and flowers come from one stem of nasturtium, a careful gardener can lift up the draped "nasties" and plant bulbs underneath.

You will be rewarded for your careful camouflaging when autumn comes. *C. autumnale* and *C. speciosum* produce large, pale lilac flowers—without leaves—*C. autumnale* in late summer and *speciosum* a few weeks later. It is probably the delicate color and the absence of foliage that led to all the "naked" names. (*Lycoris squamigera* is also sometimes called Naked Lady, so you could put a few of those in the Nudist Colony, too.) Some colchicums produce a succession of flowers, so blooming time can go on for quite a while.

Another colchicum caveat: bury your corms where the following spring you can cope with the Little Audrey effect of the huge colchicum leaves. As Louise Beebe-Wilder wrote, the foliage "ends in a most unseemly orgy of yellow dissolution, long drawn out, and unlovely." If you absolutely cannot stand the thought of all those leaves, you can still grow colchicums and never even think about this eventuality. Just take bare bulbs and put them in a row on a windowsill. Without the benefit of water or soil they will send up lovely flowers like magic. Children and adults will be amazed at your bulb-power, but don't expect a repeat performance next autumn. Dispose of the bulbs carefully (remember *mort-au-chien,* etc.) and buy new bulbs next year.

Still, many gardeners find that good planning can cover up the reality of colchicum leaves, and Vita Sackville-West did not hesitate to advocate them even for small gardens. In a tiny space where one wanted as much color as possible, she recommended Winter Jasmine, evergreen barberries, anemones, a hedge of 'Rosa Mundi', brightly colored annuals, and "filling every odd corner with things like the September/October colchicums [and] the little pink and white cyclamen."

In a larger garden colchicums are very pretty naturalized in grass. Like puschkinias, they have a seed coating that ants like to eat, and these tiny creatures will carry the seeds to their nests, lick off the coating without harming the embryo inside, then discard the seeds outside their nests. This means that your colchicums will spread nicely, perhaps after years gradually attaining the size of a Nudist Nation. Aunt Mary will be thrilled.

Colocasia: Araceae

C. ESCULENTA—ELEPHANT'S EAR, TARO, DASHEEN, KALO, EDDO

After a brief visit to other shores, the reader journeys once again to the tropics for the third and final plant in the Never-Say-Never series. It is not coincidental that part of the problem with the Three Cs (caladium, canna, and colocasia) lies in their tropical origins: temperate-zone gardeners tend to ignore plants from these regions because they imagine them to be too much trouble (untrue) or too gaudy (also untrue). Gardeners from "regular" climates (anyplace temperate) have unrealistic opinions about tropical gardens. They imagine that tropical garden design entails little more than a run through one's private bit of jungle with a machete. The plants seem foreign, dangerous, huge, entangled, and dripping with too many oddly shaped, garishly colored flowers that clash with one another. But this tropical bad dream is further from reality than Tarzan.

Tropical gardens are based on designs from ancient civilizations in India and Asia, as well as on the same European traditions that influence gardens everywhere else. There are manicured tropical gardens and those with slightly looser style, but far from being a cacophony of screaming clashers, most tropical gardens feature a symphony of greens combined with cool, calm colors.

Once educated to the possibilities, temperate gardeners find there is plenty of room for a few tropical pleasures in almost any garden. *Colocasia esculenta* is a big tropical. Each leaf rises individually from the underground part of the plant, and can grow as tall as seven feet. The leaf is usually smooth-textured with "fold marks" to add interest, and colors range from forest green to bluish black. This plant is one of several with the nickname Elephant's Ear, and the vote from here is to give Colocasia claim to the name. To watch the huge leaves wave in a gentle breeze really does remind one of majestic pachyderms surveying the savannah, standing motionless except for the gentle swaying of their alert ears.

Colocasia is one genus (as is *Caladium*) in the large Arum Family *(Araceae)* and claims six out of the more than 2,000 species included. These six produce tubers

Doug Ruhren has planted a majestic herd of Elephant's Ear (**Colocasia esculenta**) *in his garden in Durham, North Carolina.*

Colocasia adds interest to this green Charleston, South Carolina, garden.

and corms and are mostly native to tropical Asia. The genus name comes from *kolakasia,* a word for the edible root of another plant, and *esculenta* means "edible."

Another name for *C. esculenta* is Taro, a very early introduction to Hawaii. Hawaiians (the people themselves were also introductions, as the islands were originally bare, uninhabited lava cones) learned to boil or bake the root like a potato. Eventually they refined their recipes to include pounding and fermenting Taro roots into "poi." Poi has a mixed reputation in the culinary world, but, like grits, probably goes down much easier with some kind of sauce or gravy. But before you gear up for a luau complete with homegrown poi, keep in mind that the roots contain calcium oxalate crystals, which will cause intense pain if improperly cooked and ingested. Keep your Colocasias in the garden, not on the grill.

But plenty of the world's population does eat Colocasia. The roots are a popular item in Hong Kong, where they are called yams, and the foliage is also eaten by other people in the Pacific. David Fairchild, plant explorer and author of a fascinating autobiography, *The World Was My Garden,* visited Madeira in 1906 and, in a market near Camacho, saw tubers of *C. esculenta* "boiled and ready for immediate consumption," a turn-of-the-century fast-food concept.

Colocasia is very easy to grow, provided one can give it seven months of warm weather to reach maturity. This plant is another "Stay Alive at 55," and must have that temperature as its nighttime minimum. During the day Colocasia needs at least 65 to 70 degrees to be happy. People in the South should have no problems with these requirements; people in the North may need to jump-start the season a bit with a pot kept indoors. Like other warm-weather lovers, Elephant's Ear will hate you in a big way if you let the frost touch it.

But do put this plant on your "between the frosts" list, because few plants will give you such huge rewards for so little work. There are dryland Taros for the ground, and wetland Taros for pools and tubs full of water. Use them as specimen plants or create a herd of Elephant's Ear, but certainly try them for the pure fun of it. A dose of tropical insouciance can add just the right touch to a garden that verges on the staid, and once you grow one Never-Say-Never, there is no going back.

Crocus: Iridaceae

&

C. CHRYSANTHUS · C. SPECIOSUS—AUTUMN CROCUS · C. VERNUS—
DUTCH CROCUS

Bulb booster E. A. Bowles wrote the authoritative text on *Crocus* in 1924, *A Handbook of Crocus and Colchicums*. Aside from the wealth of information it contains, Bowles's devotion to the tiny crocus and its corm strikes the reader. In fact, it is for this love that the usually gentle "Gussy" Bowles is willing to resort to bloodletting.

The "chief enemies of the crocus"—mice, rabbits, pheasants, sparrows, and chaffinches—are, it is clear, Bowles's enemies, too. For the small birds, he writes, "black cotton thread stretched across the beds is the next best preventative to killing the birds." Mice, he adds "need fighting in all months and by any means," and "traps baited with Brazil nuts are very useful weapons. Nor should one neglect the aid of cats, poison, virus, sunken jars or any other method of destroying the Field Vole." The squeamish reader finds Bowles's worst punishment of all reserved for corm-chomping larvae of the infamous turnip moth, the yellow underwing, and the angleshade moth. He instructs the gardener to poke a finger into the soil to make a hole, then plug the top with a nice piece of lettuce, after which "it is never long before the caterpillar finds the bait and avails itself of the provided bedchamber below it, and the inquiring finger detects a plump body at the bottom of the hole." What the inquiring finger does to that plump caterpillar body is just too awful to write about.

It is a fact that crocuses are a particular garden delicacy, and any good bulb catalogue or book will warn you of this. A 1904 edition of *Henderson's Bulb Culture* has an engraving of a fluffy bunny overlooking a crocus

Forcing crocuses for indoor pleasure is a sure cure for winter doldrums. Crocuses in a bowl . . .

*. . . and crocuses on
a window sill.*

patch while another cottontail disappears into the shrubbery—no doubt with mortal gunshot wounds. Walt
Disney has tried for years to tell Nature's story like it
is, and at one point you just have to give in and realize
that the garden can be a cold, cold place.

And even if one's best critter-fighting methods work
(peaceable types swear by liberal dustings of red pep-
per) and a lawnful of crocus blooms appears, it may still
go all for naught. Whether spring- or autumn-flowering, the crocus blooms during times marked by bad
weather: late or early frosts and snows, torrential rains,

Gardener and writer
E. A. Bowles was willing to
resort to violence to protect
his springtime crocus garden.

Crocuses often make their
appearance at times when the
garden is too cold to enjoy.

mud, and dull, gray days, any of which can easily ruin these short-stemmed darlings.

The answer to the crocus conundrum is to take the advice of Henry T. Williams, the late-nineteenth-century author who wrote about window gardening: "The crocus, which has for many ages been cultivated as an ornament to our flower gardens, can . . . be made an effective plant for . . . ordinary house culture." The easy alternative to threads, poisons, and squashing is to grow these cheery little bulbs right in your house— peaceful pots of yellow, white, purple, and striped flowers, beautifully arranged on a sunlit sill. It's a switch from the crocus-lawn mind-set, but it is certainly worth looking around your house or apartment and thinking about a pretty spot to grow some bulbs indoors. Try a kitchen window, a sunny hallway, or even a piano bench under the living-room window. *Where* you put your crocus makes all the difference. Think creatively and remember: "Focus crocus locus."

All who come to your house when your indoor crocuses are ablaze with color are going to be out of their heads with envy, and the wise praise-gatherer will be ready with a bit of lore. Reciting tantalizing pieces of the genus's fabulously long history will give the excuse for lingering near the fantastic display.

The Genus *Crocus* is a member of *Iridaceae,* the Iris Family. Although there are seventy-five to eighty species, the entire genus was named after its most famous species, the Saffron that is one of the autumn-blooming crocuses. Saffron was a very important plant in antiq-

uity, and in ancient Eastern languages in which only the consonant sounds were written, this flower was *k.r.k.m.* As vowels gained importance, the name became *karkum,* then *kurkum,* and eventually the Greek *krokos,* which was latinized to *crocus.* Although today *Crocus* is a generic name, these ancient names applied specifically to *Crocus sativus,* the Saffron Crocus.

Saffron was used as an artistic motif more than 4,000 years ago and was sacred to the Minoans. Religion and reproductive power were closely intertwined in those days, so there's no real subtlety in the fact that the Greek god of marriage, Hymen, wore saffron-colored drapes. The Greeks regarded the astringent scent of saffron as a perfume, too, and there is a sensual reference to this in *The Clouds* by Aristophanes. At a banquet given during Nero's reign, the floors were strewn with sawdust mixed with saffron, vermilion, and powdered mica to provide a festive cushion of perfume, color, and glitter for sandaled feet.

Hedonism aside, Saffron has had more practical uses than any other plant except flax. It provides dyes, flavor, and cosmetics, and was sometimes used by impoverished monks to replace gold leaf in religious paintings. Of course, a plant this ancient also had countless horrifying medicinal uses, one of them a prescription to cure jaundice that starts with an ounce of saffron, a quart of earthworms, and a peck of snails.

After its English introduction in 1339, Saffron became a major economic crop in that country. *Crocus sativus* was grown by farmers known as "croakers" in the area that eventually became known as Saffron-Walden in Essex. When the Elizabethan geographer and historian Richard Hakluyt visited Essex, he recorded that the croaker was becoming a dying breed, and recommended that saffron-growing should be revived.

But for all its wonderful history, the Saffron is not a good bet for your indoor crocus garden. It's tricky to grow, and you would need to have more than 4,000 before you could collect enough stigmas to make a mere ounce of saffron. Homemade saffron rice just isn't worth all that trouble, and besides, your indoor crocus garden is about charm, not crops.

The spring-flowering crocuses should certainly be in your collection. These bulbs are associated with St. Valentine, because they are supposed to bloom by February 14, and they were once a symbol for youthful gladness, inspiring poetic types to write things like "The crocus bursts upon us in a blaze of colour like the sunrise of the flowers" (Forbes Watson, in *Flowers and Gardens: Notes on Plant Beauty*).

But much earlier, when in myths everyone from shepherds to queens changed into a tree or a flower as quickly as people today change their moods, Crocus was an impetuous adolescent unable to cope with a raging case of hormones. He was smitten with a beautiful nymph and became so impatient for her love that he turned into a crocus flower. The nymph promptly turned into a yew tree. Like many of the old myths, the moral of this tale has been lost through the ages.

What *is* relevant to today's indoor gardener is that

The autumn-blooming **Crocus speciosus,** *planted in September, will flower almost immediately.*

crocuses can be grown in small containers without employing the elaborate cold frames or greenhouses that gardeners of the past sometimes possessed. As with all other horticultural efforts, you will get more pleasure if you start on a very small scale with as few as a dozen corms, then expand operations as your expertise grows.

Ordinary crocuses, both spring- and autumn-flowering are a cinch to force, but will look ordinary unless you put a bit of thought into what you put them into. Green plastic pots are fine for storing the bulbs during their cold treatment time (they stack nicely in the refrigerator—but why put all that work into growing an indoor crocus garden just to end up with rows of plastic pots in your living room? A plastic pot is like a girdle: it works best when covered by something else. So slip your plastic pot into other, more whimsical containers, cover the top of the soil with moss or potpourri, and everyone will think you had the *je ne sais quoi* to grow crocuses in your auntie's priceless old Minton fruit bowl.

In earlier days there were special crocus pots for indoor gardeners. These were often shaped like beehives, hedgehogs, or porcupines and had holes through which the poor crocuses, probably embarrassed to death, poked their flowers. In 1873, Edward Sprague Rand wrote: "Crocus are often grown in fancy china pots representing porcupines. They are planted so that the leaves may represent the quills of the animal. . . . The great difficulty is to produce an even growth, the effect being a porcupine with quills in a very dilapidated condition; and therefore this mode of growth is not as popular as formerly."

Even the more modern urn-shaped crocus pot has its problems, as, with watering, the soil tends to run out of the holes, leaving pot and flowers near the bottom dripping with mud. Looking at about a millenium's worth of crocus pots, it's hard to spot a graceful design, but who knows, there may be the best crocus pot in the world in your grandmother's attic. Ask her.

There are countless alternatives to crocus pots. Open wooden flats of clean white sand (not from the salty ocean) or shallow boxes of soil work admirably. You can display the crocus box as is, or, when the flowers

Dry **Crocus speciosus** *by tying in tiny bundles, then hanging upside down.*

come into bloom, you may gently extricate them and replant in moss-lined baskets to make a hanging crocus garden.

Another method of crocus growing is to force them in water. This is best for the more vigorous bloomers such as *Crocus vernus,* the Dutch Crocus, and many catalogues offer tiny crocus glasses for this type of culture. Try these crocus glasses, but don't confine yourself to them. Use any small, watertight container—a little bud vase, a doll's teapot—on which the corm can balance and dangle its roots into the water below.

Although one old Victorian codger dryly commented that when it came to water culture, "one or two seasons generally satisfy the enthusiast," there is nothing quite as entertaining as an arrangement of tiny vases—some china, others clear to show webs of roots—each topped by a brown corm sprouting its colorful flowers.

Put your corms in soil in early September, and be sure to plant some pots of autumn-flowering *Crocus speciosus* that will provide instant gratification. Brent Heath of the Daffodil Mart suggests planting layers of bulbs, (whether spring- or autumn-blooming) in a pot—this way more can be squeezed in, and they come up in waves of flowers. Place the uppermost at least three inches under the soil, as new corms form on top of old

ones. If you keep your crocus going year after year, the babies will eventually push themselves right out of the soil in a botanical version of the animal-world mystery of lemmings rushing into the sea.

Once you've planted your corms, water them well. Keep them as cool and as dark as possible. This means the basement or garage, or if you live in a small apartment, the refrigerator. (This is when plastic pots come into their own.) After six weeks you can bring them into a cool, light place that doesn't get direct sunlight or fall below 50 degrees at night. When the buds appear, give the plants more sun. Your first pots will bloom by Christmas. You can keep pulling others out of the cool for subsequent blooming.

Don't let the fun stop when the flowers start to go over. Most crocuses will dry nicely when plucked and tied upside down in little bundles. They also press beautifully. Put lots of them between layers of newspapers and slide the whole thing under a large, heavy rug. After about two weeks these can be glued around the edges of mirrors and picture frames.

If you want to keep your corms going for another season, you must let the foliage stage take place, but this looks pretty, too. The leaves, with a pale stripe down the middle, stay fresh for a couple of weeks. Eventually, when they turn brown, it's time to let the corms dry off and rest up for next year's work.

There are many, many crocus species and varieties suitable for indoor gardening. Victorian gardeners could create erudite parlor groupings of 'Charles Dickens', 'David Rizzio', 'Sir Walter Scott', 'Queen Victo-ria', Florence Nightingale', 'Lord Palmerston,' and 'Princess of Wales'. The modern grower should choose likely crocuses from reliable catalogues and ask if they are suitable for indoor culture. Start with the absolutely easiest ones and graduate to more unusual types. Then Bowles's book, for all its ruthlessness, is the best place to look for information on specific crocuses you'd like to try.

Having followed directions, allow yourself to have some real creative fun. Use your pots, boxes, baskets, glasses, and vases of crocus to create a crazy little indoor garden. Experiment with groupings and include garden architecture and ornaments such as old bird's nests, doll's furniture, seashells, children's blocks, train-set props, or anything else you enjoy looking at. Other plants—other flowering bulbs, cut flowers, topiaries, wintering-over geraniums, ripening foliage from earlier bulb forcing—will add variety to the mise-en-scène. Then, for heaven's sake, ask people over to look at it. Winter can be such a dreary time, and a peak of bloom in your eccentric little garden is bound to amuse even the weariest of your friends. It's the perfect remedy for a crocus farmer's (croaker's) midwinter blues.

Just remind the pushiest and most envious visitors that—unlike outdoor gardens—this one is off-limits for gathering a few flowers to take home. If anyone thinks you are being selfish, just tell him or her to heed Ovid: Proserpine was picking "graceful crocus and white lilies when she was carried off." You'd be so sorry if your friend sneaked, picked, and ended up you-know-where.

Cyclamen: Primulaceae

ॐ

C. PURPURASCENS—SOWSBREAD · C. COUM—SPRING CYCLAMEN ·
C. PERSICUM—FLORIST'S CYCLAMEN ·
C. HEDERIFOLIUM—BABY CYCLAMEN

*T*he bad news about cyclamens is that they have been extensively collected in the wild, almost to the point of extinction in some of their native habitats. Twenty years ago Alice Coats wrote that *C. coum,* named after the Turkish island of Cous, had already become extinct on that island. The good news is that cyclamen are now "Born in the USA," and thanks to the hard work and far-sightedness of a few dedicated growers, modern gardeners can enjoy guilt-free species *Cyclamen.*

The genus is rather small, with about fifteen species native from Central Europe through to the Mideast. The flowers, some fragrant and some not, rise from large cormlike tubers. Although at least one species, *C. persicum,* has been very important in the indoor flower trade, other species are shade-loving, hardy, perennial flowering delights for the home garden.

Species hardy enough for outdoor cultivation are much daintier than those in the florists' shops, but they have the same reflexed flower form. It's hard to get the description of cyclamens just right. Miss Earle said they "lay their ears back like a vicious horse," and although this description does command attention, cyclamens are too cute to be compared to nightmarish creatures. Some writers compare the flowers to butterflies and moths, but these similes are far overused. Vita Sackville-West's "little frightened cyclamen" is evocative, but one might argue that it misses out on the gaiety of a pretty cyclamen colony. So in an attempt to invigorate the floral imagery pool, it will be bravely offered, at some risk,

After pollination, cyclamens protect their heir-apparents inside a tight pin curl that winds itself close to the soil.

that the reflexed flowers look like tiny flying nuns in pastel habits.

The genus name comes from *kyklos,* meaning "circle." The flowers have a whorled appearance and the tuber is rounded, but undoubtedly the most interesting circles happen after the flowers are pollinated. Then the scape start to snake themselves into perfect, firm little coils like old-fashioned pin curls. The fruits-to-be are safely wrapped inside the coils, cuddled back down to earth and nestled under the leaves.

Cyclamen were once medicinally useful. Apuleius, a second-century Roman writer, recommended that bald men who wished to restore their hair "take this same wort and put it into the nostrils." (Apuleius is remembered as a philosopher and a satirist, and surely one would need to embrace both fields to recommend, or endure, such a humiliation.) Theophratus recorded its use in preparations to treat boils and wounds, and much later, the Elizabethans thought it useful for inducing childbirth. The Elizabethan herbalist and gardener Gerard prevented pregnant women from even stepping over his cyclamen patch, so the plant must have been considered very strong medicine indeed.

Gerard grew both *Cyclamen hederifolium* and *C. coum;* the latter had been around long enough for him to report that it grew wild in Wales, Lincolnshire, and Somerset. (Actually these wild ones were garden escapees.) Parkinson grew ten kinds, including double-flowered varieties.

There are at least three classic species of *Cyclamen* that are suitable for many American gardens, and one that is nice for indoor cultivation. Elizabeth Lawrence grew all the hardy ones, with her *C. purpurascens* (syn. *europaeum*) blooming in late summer, the *hederifolium* (syn. *neapolitanum*) in autumn, and *C. coum* in winter.

William Turner (1508–68), called the Father of English Botany because he was the first to attempt systemization of British flora, wrote in 1551 that he had not seen cyclamen in Britain yet, but had heard that their name in France was "sowsbread." For efficiency's sake he proposed using the same unfortunate name in England, so that is how this weird soubriquet came to be Anglicized. In France the name was actually *pain de porceau,* because it was eaten by the wild boars in the South of France and in Turkey. Reginald "The Moraine Ma-

Nancy Goodwin of Montrose Nursery sells only cyclamens that she has raised from seed.

Cyclamen persicum *blooming in winter at the* Cloisters in New York City.

gician" Farrer found sowsbread distasteful and proposed "food of the gods" instead. In Italy they have an even prettier name, *patate della Madonna,* and the Swiss call them *alpine violets,* but no matter how nicely they are named in other languages, the fact remains that these cyclamens were called sowsbread in English.

Mrs. Beeton, the Julia Child of Victorian cookery, wrote that in France, the pig's diet of cyclamen tubers gave a special flavor to the pork of Périgord. (This is believable, because it is also true of the peanut-fed pigs grown in Tidewater Virginia that become Smithfield hams.)

In the language of flowers, if one received a bouquet of cyclamens it signified "goodbye," and even to dream of cyclamens signified catastrophe. Perhaps if the receiver were a Périgord pig this might make a little sense, but to connect a tussy-mussy of cyclamens with disaster seems odd.

Today people grow *C. purpurascens* because it has rosy, fragrant flowers. Nancy Goodwin, who started Montrose Nursery with "the primary purpose of producing all the cyclamen species from seed and making them available growing in their containers," rather than selling bulbs collected in the wild, reports that this Cyclamen is among the hardiest species, but that it may be a little slow to establish. After you make sure there are no wild boars in your area, there is nothing to do but to plant and be patient. The wait is surely worth it.

C. coum is the so-called Spring Cyclamen that flowers between December and March. It is hardy to zero degrees, and has been known to produce ready-to-flower buds during its first winter while growing under a mulch of ice-covered pine boughs. The species is certainly pretty, but perhaps not to be attempted in areas where awful weather makes it impossible to be in the garden from December to March. That's a bit like putting your candle under a bushel. But if you live in an area where the winter garden is a still, magic place, nothing could be more special than quiet little corners of *C. coum.*

Another winter-blossoming cyclamen is *C. persicum,* the old Florist's Cyclamen. This is a tender species unsuitable for outdoor cultivation in most parts of the country, but it has been a favorite indoor bloomer since its introduction to Britain in the early 1700s. In the 1760s, John Bartram, the Quaker plant collector who began America's oldest surviving botanic garden in Philadelphia, wrote to his European friends, hinting that he would appreciate some "plants for winter diversions." Soon his hand-built cool greenhouse had a white *C. persicum* and, from his special plant-exchange friend Peter Collinson, "a blue cyclamen."

Victorian nurserymen made *C. persicum* very popular from the 1860s onward, but as the florists bred this species to make bigger and bigger flowers the scent disappeared, and gradually, so did a lot of its grace. Thankfully, it is still possible to attain the species *C. persicum,* and to rediscover why Mrs. Beeton lovingly called these plants "floral bijous."

Of all the lovely cyclamens, *C. hederifolium* is the Beginner's Cyclamen, an autumn bloomer suitable for

C. hederifolium *is a hardy cyclamen, perfect for beginners, that blooms in autumn. Here grown by William Lanier Hunt at the Hunt Arboretum in Chapel Hill, North Carolina.*

gardens through zone 5. Its flowers vary in color from pink to white, and its leaves may vary. Mr. Bowles (who had tubers at Myddleton House almost half a century old!) wrote: "It is difficult to find two plants on which the leaves are identical in shape and also in the pattern of their wonderful silvery markings. In outline they are circular, triangular, rounded or heart-shaped, with either plain or toothed margins, and many have pointed lobes like those of ivy. Other types are long and narrow, like lances or arrowheads. I have some plants with leaves glossy and dark green all over, others with wide silvery margins around very dark green central botches, and a few almost suffused with gray and silver."

Another surprise is that this delicate little flower is so undemanding in its culture. Tubers of *C. hederifolium* start out modestly but willingly spread and make a nice colony of little flying nuns zooming watchfully over crisp fallen autumn leaves. This cyclamen prefers poor dry soil, and although the roots form mostly on top of its tubers, do not plant them too deeply. It's also a bad idea to move the tubers around. They will get bigger, but increase slowly by seeds instead of offsets, so there is little chance of overcrowding (in your lifetime).

C. hederifolium looks lovely in lots of garden settings. In her book on ground covers, English garden writer Margery Fish features a black-and-white photograph of the white flowers and dark leaves of the Hellebore 'Eva' among the marbled leaves of *C. hederifolium*. Elizabeth Lawrence grew them "in a few yards of space," and it is even possible to grow them where there is no garden at all. The tubers can be grown outdoors on terraces in boxes of loamy soil, as long as dappled shade is available.

But perhaps the prettiest way of all to grow cyclamens is to copy the connoisseurs of North Carolina. Nancy Goodwin and William Lanier Hunt have flocks of low-flying cyclamens sweeping through their hardwood forests. Anyone who sees those tiny pale silky flowers against the crinkled brown tree leaves will agree with a dear gardening friend of Mr. Hunt's, Elizabeth Lawrence, who wrote: "Goes to show that the gardener who thinks that the little bulbs bloom only in spring is missing the best of them."

Fritillaria: Liliaceae

❧

*I*n 1936, Louise Beebe Wilder devoted an entire chapter of her book *Adventures with Hardy Bulbs* to the fritillaries, but with a warning: "Fritillary is the problem child of the Lily family. I was on the point of saying the bad child, but bad children are not recognized in modern child psychology—only unadjusted ones."

In this burst of petulance the usually genial Mrs. Wilder betrays a sentiment shared by gardeners: she had simply had it with fritillaries because no one seems able to talk about the genus without dwelling forever upon one unlovely plant. The ancient *Fritillaria imperialis* was the first plant mentioned in Parkinson's *Paradisi*. It is well known that the Elizabethans were attracted to odd plants, and with its shaggy topknot of harshly colored, bad-smelling flowers the Crown Imperial earned a place in their hearts and gardens. Perhaps it would not appear so jarring if it bloomed later in the year in a full border of lush, perfumed flowers. But somehow it always seems to tower over the bare earth and smaller spring bulbs like a gawky adolescent out to impress a playground full of preschoolers. Although many old books call it "the grandest of all spring bulbs," the Crown Imperial has a lack of grace that makes it awkward even in an "anything goes" cottage garden.

Even gardeners who try their best to avoid this awkward old-timer have had to live with it. One beginner city gardener, wanting to grow the dainty Checkered Lily, *F. meleagris,* in her small garden, accidentally ordered fifty Crown Imperials and "the following spring was overwhelmed by their odor—decidedly over-

Checkered Lilies **(F. meleagris),** *come in purple and white and subtle white-on-white.*

Tall, dark, and handsome
Fritillaria persica *in the*
Whiteside–Hales garden.

*Dangerously over-collected in the wild, **F. persica** is not difficult to propagate in the garden.*

powering in a walled city plot." Although Clusius was proud that "I grew it in my little garden in Vienna in 1580," standards of olfactory acceptance have risen substantially since those odoriferous old days. *Caveat emptor!*

But for every brash, overpowering child in a family, there is usually one and sometimes two really nice children waiting to please. *Fritillaria* is a genus widely distributed in the Northern Hemisphere, with about one hundred species native to Europe, Asia, North Africa, and western North America. New species have been introduced as recently as the 1960s, but if it is antique species you want, there are some lovely, easy-to-grow fritillaries.

Mrs. Wilder called *F. meleagris,* the Checkered Lily, "the white hope" of the family because it almost always "endures and increases." This tiny native of Europe is so graceful and delicate-appearing, and its purple-and-white checks so distinct, it's impossible not to be astonished by its beauty. This is the "plaid-clad punk ballerina" of *Antique Flowers;* it is definitely one of the good children to have in your garden.

But our subject here is another good, largely unpraised child of *Fritillaria,* the tall, dark, and handsome *F. persica.* Unbeloved in the past for its unusual color, many modern gardeners are falling for its hardiness, striking form, and sweet perfume. If *meleagris* is the delicate dancer of the genus, *persica* is the prince.

F. persica (syn. *arabica, eggeri, libanotica*) was introduced to English gardens in the late sixteenth century, around the same time as *imperialis*—but "Old Stinky" fascinated everyone so much for so long that no one has really yet taken up the banner for *persica*. (Maybe blondes *do* have more fun.) Although a few writers describe *F. persica* as brown, E. A. Bowles's description is much closer: "The glaucous leaves suggest weathered copper greened with age and the flowers are like bronze bells wrought by some Japanese artist." Margery Fish, a champion of flower underdogs, described their color as slate blue "like a thundery sky." The flowers are a lovely deep violet blue. The majestic and stunning cultivar 'Adiyaman', which can grow to a stately forty-eight inches, has a sweet, unobtrusive scent, a matte finish on its light-colored leaves, and dark flowers.

Another sterling characteristic of this bulb is that it is reliably hardy everywhere in this country except where summers get extremely dry and hot. In fact, during a recent terrible bulb winter, when alternating warm and cold temperatures and a lack of snow caused many bulbs to take the spring off, *F. persica* seemed totally unfazed and bloomed bravely among the equally reliable Grape Hyacinth, *Muscari armeniacum*.

Perhaps one reason many authors fail to mention *F. persica* is that, until very recently, it was difficult to obtain. Today it is often available from reputable sources, but it is good to know that the few-scaled bulbs, such as fritillaries, are also not difficult to propagate in one's own garden. Grow *F. persica* a few seasons, then carefully dig up what you have in early autumn and break off the outside scale. Plant these babies immediately (they will die if they dry out). Martyn Rix says that the "inner scale will probably flower as well as if it had not been touched, the outer one will make a flowering-sized bulb next year." Don't try this every year; let the bulbs settle back in for a few seasons before digging them up again. It would be far better to create your own *F. persica* nursery bed than buy them from a dealer who sells bulbs collected in the wild. If you do buy *F. persica,* make a point of asking for sources; bulb conservationists suspect that this plant is often harvested from the wild.

E. A. Bowles wrote: "*Fritillaria persica* exists, but without happiness." It is up to those who have had enough of the overbearing fritillary child to grow and then sing the praises of *persica,* the prince. It couldn't happen to a nicer guy.

Hemerocallis: Liliaceae

❧

H. LILIOASPHODELUS—LEMON LILY, YELLOW DAYLILY · H. FULVA—
TAWNY DAYLILY, ORANGE DAYLILY · H. MINOR—DWARF
DAYLILY · H. CITRINA—NIGHT-BLOOMING DAYLILY

There is nothing more satisfying than converting someone to one's own way of seeing things. The Inquisition, wars, tent revivals, and newspaper editorial pages all attest to the popularity of persuasion throughout history.

Gardeners are no different: we keep up a continual barrage of persuasive tactics with each other, ranging from the subtle "Those roses would look beautiful against that gray stone wall" to the direct "Get up and get your spade; we're moving these now." People who would never presume to give a personal gift, for example a sweater or perfume, think nothing of giving someone pots and pots of plants meant to be permanent additions to that friend's garden—often an area the recipient gardener cares much more about than her wardrobe or living room.

But there are plants that challenge even the most potent evangelists. Begonias instantly spring to mind, and, daylilies, unfortunately do, too. One potential convert recently declared that she had dug up *all* her daylilies and fed them to the cows. Which just goes to show the challenge quotient can rise substantially with some plants.

But for every side of the fence, there is always the other—and although being a mugwump may be the safest course, sitting on the fence gardenwise is just too boring even to contemplate. Herewith, an abbreviated propaganda sheet on daylilies. . . .

Daylilies are fascinating. They are among the oldest cultivated plants known to man and were once important both for food and medicine. In the Far East the flowers were gathered and eaten as a delicacy, a practice that continues today as creative cooks with an eye on the past use the large, colorful, trumpet-shaped flowers in salads and soups.

The ancient Chinese called the Orange Daylily the Plant of Forgetfulness: they believed that eating one had so potent an intoxicating effect you would be cured of your sorrow through forgetting the cause. Any analyst today will tell you this route to happiness is a big mistake that will cost you zillions of dollars in therapy over the next five years. By all means, put the flowers in your soup, but there are surely better ways to work out your feelings.

The genus has about fifteen species which are mostly native to Central Europe, China, and Japan. The roots look like clusters of miniature sweet potatoes. Daylilies should be a gardener's dream: they are extremely easy to grow in either sun or partial shade and in moist soil or dry, they are disease-resistant, and they are free-flowering. Indeed, daylilies are survivors. Along with lovely

The ancient Chinese called the Tawny Daylily the Plant of Forgetfulness. The name remains appropriate today as this flower can be totally forgotten and will still flourish. Jan Cowles's garden, Long Island, New York.

❧

A tall, autumn-blooming daylily at Wave Hill, New York.

Yellow daylilies and blue echinops in a summer border at the Frelinghuysen garden in Massachusetts.

old roses, they are the flowers we often see blooming bravely in old, abandoned gardens, years after the gardener has moved on. Although their name means "beauty for a day" (*hemera,* "day," and *kallos,* "beauty"), with planning one can enjoy a succession of daylilies from May through September. Many of them are perfectly hardy throughout the entire mainland U.S.A., so unless you repeatedly mow them to pieces

wildly popular in the first place. Getting right back to basics usually prods the memory, and with daylilies, it is the older species that have captured gardeners' fancies century after century. Four that anyone should try are the venerable *H. lilioasphodelus* (syn. *H. flava*, 1596), the Lemon Lily; *H. fulva,* the lovely old Tawny Daylily (1596); the petite *H. minor* (1759); and the not-quite-century-old night-blooming *H. citrina* (1902).

H. lilioasphodelus is the pretty Yellow Daylily included in *De Materia Medica* of the first century A.D. Later, in the sixteenth century, Gerard wrote that he had them in his garden but noted that they did not grow wild in England. Throughout the 1600s they were very widely grown in both Old World and New, and they were a special favorite in early American cottage gardens. The Lemon Lily was a popular dooryard flower in New England, along with other Elizabethan favorites such as crocuses, tulips, hyacinths, daffodils, irises, peonies, and Lilies-of-the-valley. In old books and diaries you might see two other monikers for these garden classics. Custard Lily or Liricon-fancy, a name also shared with Lily-of-the-valley in England, and the Yellow Tuberose, on account of their beautiful perfume, which is reminiscent of that flower.

Louise Beebe Wilder described the scent of the Lemon Lily as "light, fine, and a little fruity," and for this and its lovely form it is perfect for bringing indoors. The flower stem rises about three feet, and eight to ten yellow trumpets will sound from each head. Lemon Lilies bloom in midspring, and the Victorians combined them in huge flower arrangements with red and white peo-

(or feed them to livestock that may have very good reasons for wanting to forget), once you have daylilies they are going to bloom for you. They are as fail-proof as any living thing can be expected to be.

Some tuned out daylilies about five years ago when these flowers, along with ornamental grasses, became faddish—and fads can become so overwhelming one tends to forget the reasons why the faddish item became

Country roads and daylilies were meant for each other. Oscar de la Renta's Connecticut garden.

nies. As with other daylilies, simply refrigerate buds picked in the morning and they will open wide just in time to make beautifully scented dinner-party decorations. The perfume and the cheerful yellow blooms can also be enjoyed off-season, as this and other daylilies do not mind being dug out of their winter beds and potted up for indoor forcing.

There are small daylilies suited for pot culture on balconies and terraces. This is a modern cultivar ('Bitsy') found in the magnificent autumn border designed and maintained by Edith Eddelman and Doug Ruhren for the North Carolina State University Arboretum in Raleigh, North Carolina.

Gerard gave 1596 as the introduction date for *H. fulva,* which may have arrived from Japan along the old spice routes. By Gerard's time, it was being used medicinally to treat mastitis. It came to the New World with the settlers and is now so widely naturalized throughout the eastern United States that many will be surprised to learn that it is not native, but introduced.

The orange Tawny Daylily has been called False Tiger Lily and, mysteriously, Eve's Thread. This Daylily is slightly taller than the Lemon Lily, having leaves up to thirty-six inches long and flowering stems that tower as tall as six feet. Some gardeners balk at *H. fulva*'s orange color, but there is a rosy-colored version that is also quite old. You can see this rosy one in Pierre Joseph Redouté's book *Les Liliacées,* which he painted between 1802 and 1816. Many believe Redouté was the most popular plant painter of all time, and he worked for the famous plant fancier Empress Josephine. He finished his work on the Lily Family just before beginning his most famous collection, *Les Roses* (1817–24).

For those who crave the unusual, there is an orange, very old double form of *fulva* that was much talked about by travelers to Japan from 1712 onward, but no one seemed to be able to get it out of that country until its European introduction in 1860. It is called 'Kwanso' Flore Pleno and is just a little too ruffled for those with simple flower tastes. However, the one with variegated foliage should especially please anyone who seeks further daylily thrills.

The mid-1700s saw the introduction of another yellow daylily, one that was, at first, considered a miniature version of *lilioasphodelus.* A botanical authority no less than Philip Miller, who was head gardener at Chelsea Physic Garden for most of the eighteenth century, recognized *minor* as a separate species, and it has remained distinct ever since. *H. minor* has grasslike foliage and fragrant yellow flowers that open in May, and those with very small gardens, or even no garden at all, will find it a well-behaved pot plant that only requires moderate sun for two seasons of bloom. (For those who enjoy perfumed flowers it is especially worth noting that many of the yellow daylilies have nice scents, while the orange ones tend to have no perfume at all.) The old cultivar 'Little Minor' blooms twice—both early in spring and late in autumn—and also smells sweetly.

Modern plant explorer Roy Lancaster, author of the enormous, beautifully photographed book *Travels in China: A Plantsman's Paradise,* wrote that in June and July, one can look out from the Great Wall of China and see the yellow blooms of *H. minor* shining bravely forth. Perhaps earlier plant explorers, too, stood upon that huge, ancient, rugged fortification to gaze out at those small, ephemeral wild flowers.

After the devout gardener has presented the potential convert with the preceding arguments, even the most diehard daylily-dreader should be convinced that his or her own garden is totally incomplete without a clump of these plants lovingly donated from your own garden. But there is one final argument you may be called to overcome. Prostrated by your nonstop praise of daylilies, dazed by daylily history, caught in the web of their wonderfulness, perhaps your almost-convert will manage to rally defenses when you leave to find a shovel. Still resisting your superior garden tastes, the near-recipient, panting from exhaustion, may still smile wanly and say, "Thanks anyway. I really don't need any daylilies, because, by the time I get home from work, they're all closed up. . . ."

At this point, whatever happens, *Do not let your friend leave the garden!* Take advantage of his or her weakened state, use the shovel to barricade the garden gate, fling your muddiest tools onto the garden walk, and in your kindest, most soothing voice announce: "Didn't you know there are daylilies that open at night?" Then, pull your friend over to see yours.

Hemerocallis citrina is a fragrant, oxymoronic Night-Blooming Daylily. It was introduced around 1902, probably from China. It blooms in midsummer and is renowned for its floriferousness, sometimes producing a succession of thirty to forty blooms on one stalk. The flowers open in the evening and stay open all night, making this plant an absolute must for the commuter.

Trembling with exhaustion, your friend will now be too weak to refuse at least ten healthy clumps of various daylilies. But as you prepare to pass along your in-every-way desirable plants, this is the time to ascertain that they will be used in your friend's garden exactly as you see fit. You have not worked this hard only to see your daylilies relegated to a position just east of the compost heap.

Now is the time to drop the most possible names in the shortest time possible. Begin with famous English garden writer William Robinson, who wrote: "Few plants surpass a strong, well-flowered clump of *Hemerocallis fulva* as we have seen it mixed with a group of male Fern near a brook. The leaves . . . were overhanging the banks of the stream, intermingled with fern fronds, while the flower heads, straight and tall, were towering upwards." (Robinson's use of the royal "we" is so masterful. You can imitate this to give further strength to your words.)

Robinson's fellow countryman, designer and writer Russell Page, planted pale yellow *H. lilioasphodelus* at waterside with dark-blue Siberian Iris. Even if one has no stream or pond, a boggy area can be made quite stunning with the swanlike white necks of *Lysimachia clethroides* swooping among the upright stems of daylilies.

In other parts of your friend's garden, the leaves of daylilies would look fresh with early spring flowers, and in summer daylilies might look lovely in an all-bulb border along with camassias, eremuruses, lilies, cannas, and gladioluses. Tell your friend that Margery Fish, the champion English cottage gardener, wrote that with the addition of ferns and shade-loving bulbs, one can make a daylily shade border "that will take care of itself and present a decent appearance at all times." (If only one's children could do the same.)

There are now more than seven thousand varieties of daylilies. Be sure to grow enough to give away to friends.

Elizabeth Lawrence, you can add quickly, wrote a whole chapter on daylilies in *A Southern Garden: A Handbook for the Middle South*. She described wonderful daylily combinations: Lemon Lily with pink peonies and *Iris pallida* 'Dalmatica'; and Lemon Lily with the wine-and-faun-colored 'Ambassadeur' Bearded Iris. (The Yellow Daylilies "bring out the rich red of the falls and light up the standards.")

If these big names and big plans overwhelm your fresh convert, give this tyro a few easy ideas. Include Lemon Lilies with lupins; 'Little Minor' with the papery yellow and orange blossoms of Iceland Poppies; or early-blooming Yellow Daylilies underplanted with bright blue *Veronica teucrium*. Just planted on their own in wide swathes along the driveway, the bright yellows or oranges of daylilies can even make asphalt look prettier.

After you have shoved the last muddy clump of daylilies onto the backseat of your friend's car and slammed the door shut, lean into the driver's window and casually deliver one last piece of horticultural scholarship: "You know, you really are wise to get onto daylilies now. They are among the most highly bred border plants—the first crossings were made almost one hundred years ago. In *Plants from the Past*, David Stuart and James Sutherland say that in several hundred years collectors will be agonizing about all the vanished varieties." Now is her chance, you will tell her. There are over 7,000 varieties available. As you finish your speech, pull your head quickly out of the window and stand clear of the mud spraying up from your friend's spinning tires. She's had enough for now, but once her daylilies start to bloom she's going to see the wisdom of your ways.

Hyacinthus: Liliaceae

·❧·

H. ORIENTALIS—GARDEN HYACINTH, DUTCH HYACINTH ·
H. ORIENTALIS VAR. ALBULUS—ROMAN HYACINTH

Years ago, Flora Ann Bynum, the same Flora Ann who is one of the many live wires that make the Southern Garden History Society so popular, approached Elizabeth Lawrence with a flower question. She wanted to know the name of "a very sweet-smelling pink hyacinth with a double blossom" that was sold by farmers' wives as cut flowers in small Southern produce markets. She also wanted to know more about "the little single blue hyacinths so common to our garden here" (in North Carolina).

Miss Lawrence informed her that both were Roman Hyacinths, *Hyacinthus orientalis* var. *albulus,* a bulb from southern France. Mrs. Bynum did some digging. She discovered that the species had been been cultivated since Parkinson's time, was very popular for forcing during the Victorian era, and went into old Southern gardens who-knew-when.

Unfortunately, true Roman Hyacinth bulbs were just about impossible to buy, so unless you had them already, you probably never would. This unfairness bothered Mrs. Bynum, and she started a quickly growing grass-roots campaign to get this lovely bulb back on the market. Serendipity played a part, but within several months of the launching of her quest, the species was very much for sale, gracing the cover of an especially pretty flower catalogue. For the first time in decades, those not fortunate enough to inherit a Southern garden could have forced Roman Hyacinths wafting springlike scents all through their wintery houses. It was a sensation that many had thought would never happen again.

The old-fashioned Roman Hyacinth nearly disappeared from bulb markets a few years ago. Forced by Peggy Newcomb and photographed at Monticello.

Hortus Third says there is just one species of *Hyacinthus,* the genus having been revised many times when Grape Hyacinths *(Muscari)* and Squills, among others, left to make genera of their own. There are, however, many lovely old varieties that we can grow in our gardens, Southern or not, and all of them come with a wonderful story.

The Greek myth about the accidental death of young Hyacinthus probably has something to do with why the language of flowers adopted this one to mean "sorrow."

For those who like all their ducks in a row, it will undoubtedly cause some anguish that the mythological flower Apollo made from his young friend's spilled blood simply cannot be the hyacinth. The unfortunate youth should have been named Gladiolus; the description plainly calls for markings on the petals, and the hyacinth has never had any.

By 1629, *Hyacinthus* was "so plentiful in all gardens that it is almost not esteemed." Besides his white Roman Hyacinth, Parkinson grew three double varieties of Garden Hyacinths among others. A cult of the Garden Hyacinth grew, and by 1733 there were 2,000 varieties readily available. By the end of the century "a fine hyacinth truss had at least thirty bells," and by 1909 the average was fifty to sixty flowers to a stem. There was even one type, 'Jacques', that boasted 110 flowers on a single stem, probably becoming the first hyacinth truss to require a truss. Although many today grow such heavily laden hyacinths in their gardens with great success, their rather top-heavy, brightly colored blooms are not to everyone's taste.

It would be hard, however, to locate someone who failed to succumb to the daintier charms of the Roman Hyacinth, a plant for the "less is more" school. Seven to twelve white, pink, or blue flowers make up in sweet scent what they seemingly lack in numbers. However, each bulb will produce three to four spikes of flowers, so even one will make a nice show of green foliage and colored flowers.

The white Roman Hyacinth, which blooms earlier than the others, was one of the three most popular bulbs for forcing in Victorian times. Their culture was very simple, the results were wonderful, and according to *Henderson's Bulb Culture*, an early-twentieth-century guide, they became "very largely used for forcing by florists in all large cities." For those who do not garden in Miss Lawrence's neck of the woods, forcing is the best and easiest way to enjoy Roman Hyacinths.

For the quickest bloom, force them in water, in the Victorian tradition of the old hyacinth glasses. These were pinched-waist vases that approximated the idealized female form of the era. They were manufactured in various colors—some clear, some opaque—and were often made with three vases joined together like curvy Siamese triplets.

Today the choice of forcing glasses is more limited (and very boring), so try forcing your bulbs like crocuses on top of doll's teapots, bud vases, or any container with a smallish opening. Wedge the bulb in with a bit of moss, but don't expect it to withstand earthquakes, cats prowling, and children thundering by without toppling over. Give your pretty flower a peaceful position to properly protect it and show it off.

But before the showing-off stage, you must root your plant. If your bulbs seem dried out when they arrive, try the old method of placing them in dampened sand for a couple of days. If they begin to get a touch of mold, rescue them immediately. Then put the bulb on your container of choice and add water up to, *but not touching,* the bottom of the bulb. Place in a dark area that stays at about 50 degrees—a cool cellar or an unheated closet. Change the water twice a week by hold-

Many who find the larger Garden Hyacinth a bit too showy feel that the daintier form of the Roman Hyacinth has great charm.

ing the bulb and carefully tipping the liquid out. Replace with fresh, lukewarm water and be very careful not to break off the emerging roots or stems.

When the spikes appear they will look a bit like tiny, blanched endives. When these are two inches tall, move the vases to an intermediate bulb area that has subdued light and slightly warmer temperatures. When the buds are ready, place your treat for the eyes and nose in a position to be greatly admired.

The water-forcing method takes about a month and, once flowering begins, carries on for weeks as successive spikes of blooms appear from the same bulb. Get your timing going and keep bringing up new plants.

Bulbs that are water-forced should be discarded, so it is wise also to pot up Roman Hyacinths in soil and keep them going year after year. The culture is basically the same, but the potted bulbs just take a little longer to bring to flower. Afterward you should let their leaves ripen and, when they begin to get brown, let the whole plant go dry. But to start off, place bulbs thickly together in medium-sized pots or make up masses of small pots that hold one bulb each. (Don't be tempted to mix up the colors in one pot, because the whites come much earlier than the blues, and you'll end up with some that still need cooling and others that need subdued light.)

The top of the bulb should peep out at you and the soil should be kept moist at all times. You can keep potted and water-forced Roman Hyacinths in the same dark, cool rooting locations and also in the same, slightly warmer intermediate spots with subdued light. It's a similiar process to forcing in water, just a different medium and time frame.

Another easy way to force Roman Hyacinths is in a container of damp moss. If the glass is clear, the white roots curling through the dark green moss look like shiny Oriental cellophane noodles in a bowl of thick, dark broth.

Whatever method you choose, once the plants are brought into the light, turn them a bit each day so that they do not lean to one side. Then, as the first spikes bloom and fade, cut them off and put them in your drying basket. New spikes will emerge, and the cut ones will add interesting form and color to your other dried petals.

Roman Hyacinths are not very expensive, so if you keep a lookout for interesting, inexpensive containers, you can give a favored friend all the necessaries for an old-fashioned Roman Hyacinth forcing. It makes a unique present, and you can thank Mrs. Bynum for the great idea.

Iris: Iridaceae

🐌

I. PSEUDACORUS—YELLOW FLAG · I. FOETIDISSIMA:—STINKING IRIS ·
I. RETICULATA · I. DANFORDIAE · I. SIBIRICA—SIBERIAN IRIS ·
I. ENSATA—JAPANESE IRIS · I. XIPHIOIDES:—ENGLISH IRIS ·
I. PALLIDA—ORRIS

New York City is a place most people seem to visit at least once in their lives. The bright lights and tall buildings of this modern, secular Mecca are so overwhelming that it is sometimes difficult to imagine New York in any other time except the Big Now. But one easy way to transport yourself back to turn-of-the-century New York is to visit a few of the Big Apple's public gardens.

For real atmosphere, hire a horse and carriage and gently clip-clop through Central Park, Frederick Law Olmstead's magnificent vision of the ultimate urban park. Or visit the Frick Museum. There Russell Page designed a small, perfect garden (one of his most famous) to anchor the ethereal beauty of what was formerly one of New York City's grandest private homes.

But to really escape to the Golden Age of New York, rent a car and make a short trip to the Riverdale section of the city to visit the beautiful gardens at Wave Hill. Here you will be delivered from the noise, traffic, and hurry of the Big Apple, and if you have a good imagination, you can plop yourself down in an altogether more genteel era.

Wave Hill was a large estate originally built in 1843, and was acquired by the Perkins family around 1893. Movers and shakers such as Mark Twain, Toscanini, and Teddy Roosevelt all, at one time or another, resided there as tenants. As at any grand estate of that period, extensive gardens were laid out, developed, and cosseted on a scale that only a few are able to reproduce today. Luckily, in 1960 the family gave Wave Hill to the City of New York, and thanks to the careful attention of its first—and present—director of horticulture, Marco Polo Stufano, the grounds and gardens retain the personal atmosphere of a private American garden of the 1920s.

Today Wave Hill is open and beautiful 363 days a

Iris time at Wave Hill is an insider's treat for June visitors.

Iris 'Victorine' at Wave Hill looks as crisp as a small child in a sailor suit.

year, and although not a period piece, it is famous for its old irises, peonies, roses, and dahlias. The wild garden, the conservatory, and the flower garden contain wonderful bulbs, perennials, shrubs, and mature trees —all in a setting that seems as if it could be your best friend's wealthy grandmother's place. One wise woman of a certain age remarked, "This place is about a time when children got dressed up to go to the park."

And if all the gods and goddesses on Olympus decide that you deserve an extra-special pleasure, then Fate will have you in New York around June 1, so that you can visit Wave Hill at iris time. There you can rest and relax among irises from other eras—ruffly old flags and fleur-de-lis in every color of the rainbow. As you wander from garden to garden, these proud old beauties will toss their perfumes right at you, scents ranging from sun-ripened grapes to old-fashioned licorice. You'll be right in the midst of the Golden Age of American gardens, but on such an intimate scale it might just turn out to be your favorite New York experience.

There are lots of different irises at Wave Hill, proba-bly as nice a collection as you'd be likely to see outside a botanic garden or an iris idiot's hoardings. Here you'll begin to fathom that the Genus *Iris* has more than 200 species, divided roughly into two groups according to whether they are rhizomatous or bulbous. From there the genus becomes almost too complicated for words, so try using this abbreviated family tree to help you to figure out where different irises you'll see belong.

To add to your possible confusion, just because an iris is named German, English or Timbuktuan, it ain't necessarily so. Irises have been around for ages and everyone who ever saw them brought them home, where they grew forever and ever until everyone's descendants assumed they had always been around. And with a flower so steeped in antiquity, this is almost true.

The iris appeared repeatedly in Minoan art, the most famous example at Knossos, where a bas-relief of a young priest-king is surrounded by clearly recognizable irises.

In ancient Greece it was believed that the goddess Iris led the souls of dead women to the Elysian Fields, and

this is why the purple iris was often painted on the graves of women. The Mohammedans also associated the iris with death, and often used white irises as cemetery decorations. This great conquering people took the iris to North Africa, the Iberian Peninsula, and even as far afield as Mexico. But this was far from the iris's first trip away from home.

King Thutmose III (c. 1501–1447 B.C.) of Egypt brought back irises and other flowers from his conquest of what is now Syria. His garden was then so magnificent that he did the B.C. version of having some glossy shelter magazine photograph it for posterity: he had the flowers carved into the wall of the temple of Amon, along with a modest little statement about having, indeed, grown each one.

The use of the iris as a heraldic emblem is often attributed to a sudden flash visited upon Clovis I, King of the Franks during the fifth century A.D. While out on an international raid, Clovis and his army found themselves trapped between a larger enemy army and the wide Rhine River. Gazing out upon the impossible, Clovis saw a glint far out in the river. It was a group of irises, probably Yellow Flag (*I. pseudacorus*), a plant that he knew grew in shallow water. Eureka! Clovis's army successfully forded the river and escaped the enemy and certain death. Upon reaching terra firma on the far shore, Clovis decided upon two things he wanted to do as soon as possible: replace the three black toads on his standard with three golden irises, and renounce paganism for Christianity.

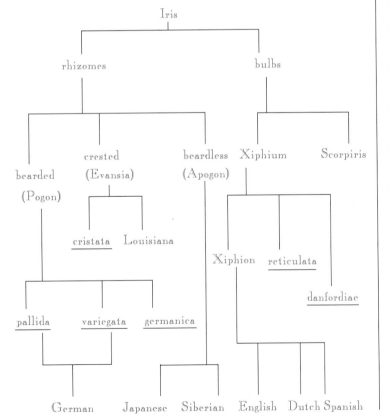

The water-loving yellow
Iris pseudacorus *saved the*
lives of an entire army.
Lady Anne Tree's garden,
Shaftsbury, England.

I. pseudacorus *in the Reuter*
family garden in Virginia.

Iris 'Chenedole' (1872) at Wave Hill.

Iris 'Othello' (1848) at Wave Hill.

Six hundred years after Clovis's conversion, his descendant Louis VII of France used the same fleur-de-lis as his standard when his army trotted off to reclaim the Holy Land for Christianity. It is no mistake that the stylized flower also resembles the hilt of a sword or an arrowhead, and the iris later became the flower of chivalry.

Its symbolic connection with religion and politics flourished when the iris gradually began replacing the Madonna Lily of the Virgin Mary in Flemish and Spanish paintings. Because the French House of Burgundy, still with the iris as its emblem, protected the Flemish artists, these painters began using the iris as their symbol. Hugo van der Goes of Ghent painted the great *Adoration of the Shepherds* that now hangs in the Uffizi Gallery and, in the foreground, included a vase with two red lilies and three irises—one blue and two white. This lead the way for subsequent painters to use the iris alone, without the lily, to symbolize the Virgin. After 1506, when the Hapsburgs incorporated Flanders and trade between Flanders and Spain increased, this custom spread to the religious art of Spain.

Today the fleur-de-lis is just another artistic device, and it is sometimes difficult to comprehend the potency this symbol had in a different era. Perhaps an equivalent heart-tugging, patriotism-rousing symbol for our own time, is the ubiquitous yellow ribbon tied around trees in front yards, wrapped around every lamppost on Main Street, and used in decorating little girls' hair.

A plant this old is bound to have interesting medicinal uses, and with irises the recipes became so elaborate that even the harvesting of the roots was a prescribed procedure. Rhizotomi, the root-digger pharmacists of ancient Greece, were required to use a double-edged sword and circle three times around the plant. The first

Purple Siberian Irises and red poppies in the Reuter's garden in Virginia.

bit of root dug up had to be held in the air with one hand while the rest of the roots were hacked out with the sword. Iris rhizomes could be harvested only by those in a state of chastity, which these days means you'd have to let your favorite frail maiden aunt wield the sword.

Once rhizomes were harvested, one of the more repeatable medicinal uses was in a concoction of iris root and wine that "fastens loose teeth if the mouth be washed therewith." If this really worked, one could forget the horrors of peridontia forever.

Orris, the violet-scented element of many perfumes and cosmetics, is obtained simply by drying the rhizomes of certain iris species for two years. This substance has been used for centuries in powder, toilet water, sachets, rosaries, and flavorings. In Germany, a piece of orris was at one time suspended in beer barrels to keep the beer fresh. In France it was added to wine to enhance the bouquet. In England orris was an ingredient in sweet, artificial brandy, and in Russia it was used in a soft drink. (Plan your trip back in time accordingly.)

In France, orris was added to flour to make the hair powder essential in constructing the elaborate hairdos of the prerevolutionary court. Other additions to these three-foot-high coifs were wool, pads, wire, false hair, ribbons, plumes, ropes of beads, artificial flowers, and glass objects including, but not limited to, birds, animals, and insects. On the other hand, French peasant women scented their bedsheets on washday by suspending several pieces of dried orris on a string into the final hot rinse. The roots could be dried and used over and

*Violet-scented orris is made by drying the rhizomes of certain species, such as this **I. pallida 'Dalmatica'**.*

Old fashioned **Iris sibirica**
'Snow Queen' under the lacy
leaves of **Rhus typhina**
'Laciniata', a fancy version
of Staghorn Sumac, at
Wave Hill.

over, and there's no reason you can't try it in a modern washing machine. Another quicker orris use is to fling a bit of root into the fire for a kind of violet-scented incense effect.

Whatever uses orris has in your house, other parts of the iris plants are useful for winter decoration. *Iris foetidissima,* fondly known as Stinking Iris or Roast Beet Plant, is unbeloved for its insignificant flowers and smelly evergreen foliage. However, this plant completely makes up for letting the side down by producing fat seedpods which burst open to display clinging "berries" (actually seeds) of brilliant scarlet, orange, white, or yellow. Gertrude Jekyll made grand dried arrangements with these (you don't dry the foliage—just the stalk and "berries"), using whole plants of Honesty with all the silvery "pennies" connected, big long branches of scarlet Chinese Lantern pods, and tall stems of Stinking Iris pods. She writes in *Flower Decoration in the House* (1907): "All these dried products of our gardens are welcome ornaments to our rooms in the early winter, though there comes a day somewhere towards the end of February when the evenings are getting longer and the days full of light, when we find our Iris berries and Chinese Lanterns shrivelled and discoloured, and, thinking of the spring flowers that are soon to come, we burn the whole thing up and are glad to be rid of it."

So after you've had a nice little bonfire of all your dried arrangements, go to the basement and begin bringing up pots of bulbous irises that you have forced for winter bloom. *I. reticulata,* a sweet little inky-blue iris (sometimes mistakenly known as Dutch Iris) is easy to come by and easy to force. Another one is *I. danfordiae,* a small yellow-flowered, sweetly scented iris introduced in 1890.

There is another winter-blooming iris grown outdoors in mild climates (zone 8 and warmer). *I. unguicularis* has a wonderful perfume when plucked and brought inside. Its nickname is Algerian Iris, and from here one can depart on a trip around the globe following the (mostly incorrect) names of other iris species.

I. sibirica, introduced before 1597, is one of our hardiest border species. The leaves are grasslike and bright green, and flowers come in white, blue, or purple. There are now rather large modern Siberian Irises, tetraploids created with colchicine, a gene-altering substance derived directly from the bulbs of colchicums. However, many favor the smaller flowered old-fashioned Siberian Irises, especially when purple ones are planted near the sweet-scented old-fashioned Lemon Lily (*Hemerocallis lilioasphodelus.*)

*Flat-topped Japanese Irises
in the Rocchia garden
in Oregon.*

Irises in the Reuter's early summer garden.

Japanese Irises are divided into species according to how much water they like. *I. ensata* (formerly *kaempferi*) was introduced in 1857 and is the one that likes to swan around on the very edge of the pond or stream. *I. laevigata* prefers to wade right in, and the design possibilities for using both types are quite wonderful.

The English Iris, *I. xiphioides,* is not English at all—however, this violet-blue flower was introduced so long ago that Clusius himself went to the British seaport of Bristol to search it out. There he found it happily growing in gardens, but search as he would, he could find none in the wild. A native of the Pyrenees, this flower took the name of its adopted country when the Dutch came to England especially to buy bulbs for their bulb trade. It was called English Iris in the *Hortus Eystettensis* of 1613, and the name has stuck ever since.

Spanish Iris is actually found in Spain, but also in France, Portugal, and Africa. *I. xiphium* enjoys a drier soil, but Parkinson managed to grow more than thirty-one kinds in his English climate. Spanish Iris was introduced prior to 1597 and was popular enough at the turn of the twentieth century for jolly old Miss Jekyll to write: "Everyone knows what capital room flowers the Spanish Iris are!"

Topping off the geographic confusion connected with this genus is *Iris germanica,* probably the oldest cultivated European iris. Now it seems that here, at last, is the grandpa of all those wonderful irises we call German Iris. But no. For some unfathomable reason, the children of *I. pallida* and *I. variegata,* of which there were at least one hundred offspring by 1840, were called German Iris. With this further bit of confusion, it's perfectly

fine if you decide to forget about trying to sort out this genus and, instead, just take a walk in the garden.

And there is no more beautiful iris garden for strolling than Wave Hill. There you will see irises dressed in pink, blue, copper, bronze, lilac, purple, white, brown, yellow, orange, and near-black. They also combine their colors in bi-tones, blends, and stipples. Furthermore, the beard of fuzzy hairs that appear on the falls (the petals the droop down) offers more colors to the scheme. These fuzzy little bumblebee welcome mats come in white, yellow, blue, brown, green, pink, shrimp, or tangerine. Then add to this sensual delight scents like sugary lemons, Lily-of-the-valley, locust trees in bloom, and old-fashioned grape Easter candy. What a walk you will have.

Because German Irises will flower two years after parents are crossed, it is only up to the imagination of the breeder what combinations of color, form, and scent will be tried. At Wave Hill there are large plantings of two-toned purple 'Fra Angelico' bred in 1926, as well as an old yellow garden hybrid called *I.* × *flavescens* that appeared around 1813. A tall yellow beauty with delicate purple veins is 'Gracchus'—bred in 1884 and a special favorite of Wave Hill gardeners. 'Chenedolle' looks very similar, but was born in 1872.

In one corner of the flower garden there is a mass of subtly combined iris colors that includes 'Cascade Splendor', 'I.M. Gedde', 'Momauguin', and 'Rosy Wings' in an antique tapestry of wines, roses, golds, and purples. In another part of the garden, a green lawn curves around a mass of clear white and royal purple 'Victorine' that looks as spiffy as a group of clean children in sailor suits.

And when you visit Wave Hill at iris time, don't forget to look up the blue wonder of *Iris pallida*. This is one of the sources of orris and is simply breathtakingly beautiful. The flower stalk rises as tall as four feet and branches to produce lots of sweet-smelling, clear-sky-colored flowers. In its native countries, this Iris is called Perunitsa, because it is the flower of Perun, the Thunder God.

In Roman mythology, Iris was the bearer of messages between Olympus and earth, and she used the rainbow as her favored method of transport. So, obviously, the next time you see a rainbow after a thunderstorm, it is a message from above: immediately run to the telephone and book your tickets to New York for end of May or beginning of June.

Once in New York, enjoy every bit of the city that you can. It'll be off-season and you'll see the Big Apple the way its residents enjoy it most. Then, one pleasant morning, accept an imaginary invitation from your best friend's wealthy grandmother, leave your hotel in your most comfortable linens, and wend your way over to Wave Hill for an idyll with the iris.

Iris was the Roman goddess who used the rainbow as her method of transportation. You may use this genus to create a rainbow in the garden —here with poppies and delphinium in the Harris garden in Philadlephia.

A collection of bronzy Bearded Irises including 'Cascade Splendor', 'I. M. Gedde', 'Momauguin', and 'Rosy Wings' add to the June glory at Wave Hill.

Lilium: Liliaceae

৵

L. CANDIDUM—MADONNA LILY, WHITE LILY · L. CANADENSE—CANADA LILY · L. SUPERBUM—TURK'S-CAP LILY · L. LANCIFOLIUM—TIGER LILY · L. REGALE—REGAL LILY · L. AURATUM—GOLD-BANDED LILY

When English essayist John Ruskin (1819–1900) considered the lilies, and how they grew, he was moved to write: "The most beautiful things in this world are the most useless, peacocks and lilies for instance."

Although a great deal of speculation had been recorded as to the identification of the Biblical lily that was arrayed better than Solomon, and that toiled not and spun not, it's now known that "lily" was formerly a catch-all term that meant *any* lovely flower. However, by the time Ruskin came along, "lily" referred to a specific genus of flowers popular enough to lend its name to a horticultural movement: the Century of the Lily (1804–1904.)

The Century of the Lily is an entirely arbitrary invention of someone who saw the period between the introduction of *Lilium lancifolium* by William Kerr, the first professional plant collector to live in China, and the discovery of *L. regale* by "Chinese" Wilson as the most exciting period in the history of the genus. It is the most relevant to today's gardening, but the Century of the Lily is only one tiny drop in the big pond known here as the Millennia of the Lily.

Dauntless plant detective Alice Coats, author of *Flowers and Their Histories,* says the Madonna Lily *(L. candidum)* "was in existence 3,000 years B.C. . . . and "it is possible that this flower is a survivor from the Quaternary Ice Age, which destroyed the plant life of most of the rest of Europe." Factually, the Madonna Lily is so old that no one knows where it originally grew because it was distributed all over Europe by very early nomadic tribes. These people would have carried the bulbs as food. It's amusing to imagine some little cave-child, not allowed to leave the fireside until he has eaten all his dinner, hiding a few bulbs under the mammoth-skin rug and thus starting yet another colony of *L. candidum.*

In ancient Greece, *L. candidum* was admired as a culinary delight and as a beautiful flower. It was the flower of Aphrodite, the goddess of love, who, like many modern love goddesses, had a big jealousy problem. She, who was born of the white sea foam, evidently felt that whiteness belonged to her, and eventually became intensely jealous of the whiteness of her flower. Rather than sully its purity, she merely added a huge pistil to the center of its bloom.

Along this line, Albertus Magnus, the great thirteenth-century scholar and theologian, wrote that one could use a lily to determine whether or not a young girl was chaste, but his specific technique went unrecorded. However, Anglo-Saxon folklore has an absolutely foolproof method of foretelling the gender of an unborn child that involves the lily. One holds a lily in one hand and a rose in the other and approaches the

*Some find the perfume of the ancient **Lilium candidum** too powerful for indoor use. These Asiatic hybrids are a bit tamer and may also be forced for indoor blooming.*

Lilies are an essential
addition to the cottage garden.
Here, modern varieties bloom
in a village garden in
Cold Spring, New York.

expectant mother. After a pregnant pause, if she chooses the rose, the baby will be a girl; if the lily, a boy. This works without fail.

In Semitic culture *L. candidum* was the symbol of motherhood, while in Christianity it represented the purity of the Virgin Mary. Because of the latter, and its medicinal uses, *L. candidum* was grown in medieval monastery gardens, though it is interesting to note that it did not get the name Madonna Lily until the nineteenth century. Before that it was simply called White Lily, a name that became confusing with the many lily introductions made in the 1800s.

One of the best places to visit authentically and beautifully recreated medieval monastery gardens is at the Cloisters, an annex of New York's Metropolitan Museum of Art. Make a Pilgrimage of Purity to see the fabulous Unicorn Tapestries (the unicorn was a symbol of chastity) and wander among beautiful, simple gardens, especially on the lookout for the Madonna Lily. In the Bonnefont Cloister, there are 250 species of plants grown in the Middle Ages for medicine, dyes, decoration, and food. Nineteen beds are laid around a fifteenth-century wellhead, and if you visit at the right time of year, *L. candidum* will shine forth in all the white glory that made it both sacred and profane for so many centuries.

In England, the dissolution of the monasteries led to a decline in plant cultivation, but as the people of the countryside became more independent, and concocted their own medical preparations from plants they grew themselves, the idea of the cottage garden was born.

Thus *L. candidum* went from the monastic garden to the cottage garden, and in later years no self-respecting cottager was without roses, and honeysuckles and White Lilies.

Unfortunately, the old cottagers seem to have had a knack for lilies that has been lost. Margery Fish, the twentieth-century chronicler of the cottage garden, wrote: "In the old days, rows of stately white lilies were a feature of every cottage garden . . . but seldom do they grow and flower with the ease and serenity as they used to. . . ." Although it is certainly worth giving this ancient lily a try, do not give up on the entire genus if *L. candidum* is too shy to make a lasting commitment to your garden. There are many, many other learner-lilies that are available, easier, and beautiful.

The Genus *Lilium* has at least eighty species and countless worthwhile cultivars. Interest in lilies as garden plants picked up in the 1600s when trade and travel increased, and lilies came to "civilization" from isolated European outposts, from China and Japan, and from the New World.

Both Parkinson and Gerard grew lots of lilies, and the former grew *L. canadense,* reporting that it had been in Paris at least nine years before he had it. This native of the eastern coast of America grows wild from Nova Scotia to West Virginia and can be found as far west as the Pennsylvania–Ohio line. It was probably originally collected by the French explorer Jacques Cartier in the very early 1600s and flowered, orangish-yellow and five feet tall, in Paris in a celebration of all the wonderful New World plants yet to come.

Another lily, the vividly colored *Lilium philadephicum* (orange-red with purple spots), originally went to France from the French colony of Acadie in about 1675 but was not successfully cultivated in Europe until 1737, when John Bartram reintroduced it to Chelsea Physic Garden.

L. catesbaei was introduced in 1788 and named for Mark Catesby, enthusiastic naturalist who spent many years in Virginia, the Carolinas, and the Bahamas. In 1729 he had a London exhibition of the first part of his drawings for the collection eventually named *A Natural History of Carolina, Florida, and the Bahama Islands*. His drawings of the exotic flora and fauna of the New World raised interest in this part of the globe to fever pitch.

Around 1727, in the London garden of Peter Collinson, *Lilium superbum* bloomed in all its orange-scarlet, up to eight-feet-tall glory. John Bartram had sent the bulb to his London plant pal, and Collinson—wealthy merchant and friend to the great Linnaeus—was so thrilled with the flower that he decided then and there to specialize in American plants.

As Collinson's American collection grew, he became an acknowledged expert on the subject, and as his desire for new plants increased, he commissioned Bartram to travel farther afield in search of the exotic. When Mr. Collinson set up a trip to Virginia for the plant-wise but unworldly Bartram, he felt it necessary to admonish his friend to "go very clean, neat, and handsomely dressed to Virginia."

But prior to the 1600s, Europeans had to content themselves with *L. candidum* alone. A few Turkish and European species and varieties were added by the end of that century, then the American introductions came on the scene in the eighteenth century. It took the first Asian introduction, *Lilium lancifolium* (introduced, and forever in our hearts, as *Lilium tigrinum*), to really begin the rage for lilies that would take place over the next century, the century of the Lily.

The Tiger Lily (one of the stars of *Antique Flowers*) was introduced from China in 1804 by William Kerr. Like *L. candidum*, the beautiful *L. lancifolium* was grown for food in its native lands, but when it was introduced as an ornamental to Europe, it became the first lily to captivate a broad English audience. Lilies from Asia became a horticultural phenomenon, and when Redouté included a large engraving of *Lis de Chine* (*L. lancifolium*) in his work *Les Liliacées,* fashionable ladies all over France swooned.

It was directly due to the widespread popularity of the Tiger Lily that further Asian plant exploration took place—which is why the Century of the Lily begins with its 1804 introduction and ends, neatly, in 1904 with Wilson's fabulous *Lilium regale*.

Lilies began pouring into Europe, but the next really big splash didn't come until 1862, when Veitch Nurseries premiered the Gold-banded Lily, *L. auratum*, at the London Flower Show. This fragrant Japanese lily with large white and yellow flowers had been unsuccessfully introduced by Dr. von Siebold, but fortune smiled upon Fortune's later introduction and *auratum* raised the Genus *Lilium* to star status.

*Lilies naturalized in Emma
Morgan's Amagansett garden.*

By the end of the century, Yokohama Nursery Company in Japan was filling millions of orders for *L. auratum*, and it was just a few years later that American plant explorer David Fairchild visited the Yokohama nursery. There he met Uhei Suzuki, its founder, and observed firsthand the mass exporting of *L. lancifolium, L. speciosum* (introduced 1832), and *L. auratum*. He wrote: "The packing sheds presented a beautiful and animated scene, peopled by a hundred or more women dressed in bright blue kimonos with figured blue and white handkerchiefs about their heads and white socks and wooden sandals on their feet. . . . The men were dressed in rather elaborate blue jackets. On the back of each was an enormous white circle in which was stenciled the company's name in Japanese characters."

It was this very company that nearly led to the end of the lily. With demand high and bulb production pushed to the maximum, weaker bulbs were bound to occur, and disease soon set in. *L. auratum* is very susceptible to lily mosaic, and *lancifolium* is a carrier of the virus, with the result that many infected bulbs were spread through Europe and America. Gardeners began suffering expensive lily losses, and soon the entire genus got a "finicky" reputation that seriously affected its popularity.

But the reputation of the lily was saved by the appearance of *Lilium regale*. The Regal Lily, for all its grand appearance, is as tough as a stocky peasant—disease resistant and one of the easiest lilies to grow, even thriving for those gardeners who brag about being neglectful. Arriving at a time when success with lilies was about as easy as teaching a peacock to plow, *L. regale* completely saved the genus from garden ignominy and to this day is one of the species lilies still widely available in catalogues. It is also one of the most widely grown of "Chinese" Wilson's introductions.

Dr. Ernest Henry "Chinese" Wilson (1876–1930) was born in England and began studying botany at the age of twenty. In 1897 he went to the Royal Botanic Garden at Kew where he decided to become a botany professor. One year after he began his program, the long tendril of fate curled down, wrapped around the budding academic, and, lifting him away from ivy-covered walls, thrust him out into a world teeming with

Many modern lilies are resistant to the viruses that plagued gardens at the beginning of this century. Caroline Burgess's planting thrives at Stonecrop in Cold Spring, New York.

undiscovered plants biding their time—just sitting and growing in every exciting, unexplored part of the world —until their European introduction.

That same tendril of fate had also wrapped around the nursery concern of Veitch & Sons, a firm that had fallen under a cloud because of its close connection with the lily disease spread by *L. auratum*. Searching for a way to reestablish his good reputation, old Mr. Veitch was inspired by Augustine Henry, a famous collector who lived in the interior of China for several years, to send a collector there in search of the beautiful, white-blossomed Dove Tree, *Davidia involucrata*.

Robert Fortune and others had been sending home Chinese plants for decades, but almost all their material came from gardens in the settled portions of the Chinese Empire. They had just about run out of new material when Veitch inquired at Kew for a hardy young man able to stand the rigors of dangerous Chinese mountain travel. The mission: to find and bring back Dove Tree seeds. Wilson stepped forward.

Veitch trained Wilson at his own nursery, and before the young man set off, gave him these final instructions: "Stick to the one thing you are after and do not spend time and money wandering about. Probably almost every worthwhile plant in China has been now introduced into Europe." Years later, after Wilson had introduced 1,500 new Chinese species into cultivation, this plant explorer proved his first boss very wrong indeed.

Wilson's first trip to China changed his life forever. He traveled by way of America and stopped in Boston

The handsome, scented **Lilium regale** *is one species that is disease-resistant and readily available on the market. It was discovered during a death-defying trip to China at the turn of this century—and now thrives in Oscar de la Renta's Connecticut garden.*

*A lily interlude in
the Cabot's white garden at
Murray Bay, Canada.*

to meet Professor Charles S. Sargent, a member of the distinguished New England family of which painter John Singer Sargent is perhaps the most famous member. Most of Wilson's time was spent in the Arnold Arboretum (many years later he became its curator) and in the Brookline, Massachusetts, garden of the Sargents. (This garden was already quite famous and was photographed about the same time as Wilson's visit and was included in Louise Sheldon's *Beautiful Gardens in America, 1915.*)

Upon finally reaching China, Wilson made an arduous and very dangerous boat journey up the Yangtze River to search for the exact location of Augustine Henry's Dove Tree. Helpful natives led him to the very spot where, many years before, Henry had first discovered the tree's large, creamy-white, birdlike blossoms. Upon

reaching the location, Wilson had a horrific shock: there in a small clearing was one big stump with a brand-new wooden hut beside it. Henry's Dove Tree would never provide seeds to take back to England.

But later on in the trip Wilson found other Dove Trees and, after a long and rewarding association, grew to know and like his Chinese helpers. His biographer, Edward Farrington, said Wilson "kept in touch with China until the day he died." Although it is said Wilson did not like the nickname "Chinese" (much as many of us dislike our nicknames, however fondly given), Farrington disagrees, writing that Wilson liked the reminder of his happy associations with the people of China.

It was on Wilson's second trip, after he had brought Mr. Veitch the seeds he so desired, that the fabulous *Lilium regale* was first discovered. In 1903, Veitch sent him back to go even farther into the interior, up through the Min River Valley, right to the Tibetan-Chinese border. This area of western China, a botanical paradise of trees, shrubs, and herbaceous plants, was, and is today, so inaccessible that photographs taken by Wilson in 1904 are accurate representations of the region as it remains in the present.

It was here, while searching for the Golden Poppy-wort (*Meconopsis integrifolia*), that Wilson discovered tens of thousands of Regal Lilies fragrantly blooming in an obscure, semiarid Min River Valley. The species was limited to this one valley, as it could not cross the encircling snowcapped peaks. Although *L. regale* would not be introduced from this trip, it was its discovery that spurred Wilson to return to China to obtain bulbs that could be introduced to America and Europe.

It wasn't until Wilson's fourth Chinese expedition, sponsored by the Arnold Arboretum in 1910, that he was able to arrange for the autumn collection of *L. regale* bulbs. This is the trip that nearly ended his life and left him with his famous "lily limp."

He traveled from Ichang to Cheng-tu and then walked 200 miles in twenty-two days to get to Sung-pan. He collected as he went—in deep gorges, beside foaming rapids, and on shale cliffs. In Sung-pan he arranged for the *regale* bulbs to be dug in October and carefully packed off to America.

On the return trip to Cheng-tu, Wilson was caught in an avalanche, and, trapped inside his sedan chair, fell hundreds of feet down a cliff. His leg was torn and broken in two places. After his helpers finally got him back on the trail and splinted his limb with a camera tripod, a long mule team appeared. The shale cliffs were still shifting and there was no room on the narrow track for the mules to turn around or for the injured Wilson to be moved to the side. Farrington wrote: "All forty mules stepped over him as he lay in the road but not a hoof touched him," but Wilson said later that "every hoof looked as big as a plate."

Wilson's leg became badly infected, but he survived to travel again. Meanwhile his Chinese assistants harvested the bulbs, loaded them onto riverboats, and saw them off on the long journey to the ships waiting at sea.

And today, every Regal Lily in our gardens is a descendant of that remarkable consignment.

Wilson proudly rested his reputation with the Regal Lily, but "he pleads with all who possess this treasure not to ruin its constitution with rich food." Those who wish to grow the Regal Lily should buy bulbs from a reputable dealer, because lilies have scaled bulbs that are fragile and easily dehydrated.

Gertrude Jekyll wrote a book on garden lilies in 1901, *Lilies for English Gardens,* and although it appeared before the Regal Lily and was aimed at gardeners in her own country, she does present some good general lily cultural advice: be very careful about planting depth, and beware of spring frosts. Some bulbs merely require planting at a depth roughly three times that of the bulb. But planting depth with lilies is crucial: some need shallow planting, as the roots spring from the base of the bulb, and others need to go in quite deep, because they also throw out roots straight from their stems. These roots actually feed the flower, so if they end up dangling in midair, the flower's growth will be stunted. Lilies with stem roots really love a rich mulch and frequent watering.

Some lilies start to push up out of the ground early in the spring and thus must be protected from late frosts. Different gardeners have various favorite techniques, but one of the easiest and best is to recycle your Christmas tree. After it has given light and cheer inside, take it outside and use its sawn-off boughs to make a protective shelter for the plants. Any little trouble you can take to have a delicious lily interlude in your garden is certainly worth the effort.

In Wilson's biography there is a black-and-white photograph taken of him in his own garden. He is dressed in a three-piece suit topped off with a wide-brimmed hat, and he is palming a cigar as a naughty schoolboy would. In his other hand, the sophisticated world traveler is holding the stem of one of his own Regal Lilies. He is peering into the many-flowered lily with a quizzical expression that sums up something he wrote in 1923: "Where does hardship figure when the reward is such?" That is a lot of mileage to get out of something that neither toils nor spins.

Lycoris: Amaryllidaceae

❧

L. RADIATA—SPIDER LILY

Almost all the old garden books that bother to mention this flower say *Lycoris* was "named after a lady in Roman history." It appears, however, that what they *meant* to say was that *Lycoris* was named after a Roman lady with a history. Modern bulb authority John Bryan reports that Lycoris was a Roman actress who was the mistress of Marc Antony.

Lycoris is rarely, if ever, seen north of the Mason-Dixon line, and in the South it is, like that Roman lady of yore, sometimes considered just a little too common. This Japanese native has settled into zones 7 and warmer with a kind of ease and fecundity that makes straitlaced people nervous. With its frilly, brightly colored blossoms and long, prominently curved stamens, *Lycoris radiata* is the lovable floozy of the Southern autumn garden.

Gardeners in the South don't need to be told about growing *Lycoris radiata*. It is something they know about when they are born. But for the unfortunates born beyond mint julep territory, it's about time they, too, became acquainted with the wiles and charms of the Spider Lily.

Like all interesting floozies, Spider Lily has a mystery in her background. For many years she lived in the South under the false and misleading alias *Nerine sarniensis*. The story behind her name mix-up involves international intrigue and the high seas.

Nerine sarniensis, Guernsey Lily, is a totally different flower from *Lycoris radiata*, Spider Lily. But Spider Lily was able to hide behind another name because she craft-ily chose an alias that already had a bit of mystery in its background.

In 1659 a Dutch East India Company ship, en route back to the Netherlands after a long sea voyage, wrecked off the coast of the Isle of Guernsey. The following year a miracle occurred: hundreds of flowers bloomed on the beach. Eventually, the resourceful islanders cultivated their gifts from the sea, calling them Guernsey Lilies, and subsequently created an important economic crop that they shipped to the London flower market.

Years later the first great plant explorer from the Royal Garden at Kew, Francis Masson (1741–1806), discovered that Guernsey Lilies bloomed all over the rocky slopes of Table Mountain in South Africa. Apparently the bulbs had been collected by Dutch East India Company sailors from the mountain slopes before their shipwreck off Guernsey. When the ship went down, the bulbs washed ashore with the rest of the cargo, fortuitously beaching on an island that provided them with perfect growing conditions.

So Masson solved the mystery concerning the birthplace and name of the Guernsey Lily. But confusions like this are never cleared up instantly, and during this period *Lycoris radiata* was able to slip into America assuming Guernsey Lily's identity. For many years she carried on with this ruse, making herself and her many offspring very comfortable in Southern gardens, but always operating under the alias *Nerine sarniensis*.

Much later, Elizabeth Lawrence became bothered by the continuation of the horticultural hoax initiated by

Lycoris and set about to get her fellow Rebs to recognize their Spider Lily for what it was. Lawrence wrote: "The nerine (here *Nerine sarniensis*) is a South African genus, and the first red spider lilies (*Lycoris radiata*) in North Carolina, and probably in this country, came directly from Japan to a garden in New Bern. They were brought to that garden by Captain William Roberts who was with Commodore Perry when he opened the port of Japan (1853). The captain brought three bulbs which were . . . in such dry condition that they did not show signs of life until the the War Between the States.

The original bulbs have increased and been passed on until they have spread across the state." *Lycoris radiata* does bear a passing resemblance to *Nerine sarniensis*. But why she chose to hide her own identity in that of another and how this farce was originally accomplished remain buried in Southern plant lore. Until someone

Lycoris radiata, *a Japanese bulb with a mysterious background, has naturalized throughout the South.*

North of the Mason-Dixon line, Spider Lily can be grown in pots and moved inside for the winter.

does further detective work or persuades bulbs to talk, *Lycoris* will just keep this secret to herself.

For now, it suffices to say that *Lycoris radiata* is a Japanese species nicknamed Spider Lily while *Nerine sarniensis,* the shipwrecked Guernsey Lily, is a South African native. Your old Aunt Belle in Raleigh will refuse to listen to this information, but it is, nevertheless, true.

Besides the Spider Lily, there are between eight and seventeen species in the Genus *Lycoris,* all native to Japan and China. One of the best-known is the pale pink *L. squamigera,* also called Resurrection Lily, Magic Lily, and most interestingly of all, Naked Lady. (This is the bulb to plant in your floral Nudist Colony with *Colchicum autumnale,* Naked Boys.)

But for gardeners north of Virginia, the fragile beauty of *Lycoris radiata,* cultivated in pots, delivers a wanton thrill that precious few flowers can muster. With a long, bare scape topped by an amazing pompon of color and frill, the Spider Lily makes a wonderful specimen plant that can be moved in and out of the house with grace and ease.

Luckily, Spider Lily's reputation for easiness also covers her pot cultivation, and the minimum of effort will produce raves from your Yankee friends. The bulbs are usually available in midsummer and should be planted immediately. Put one bulb in a five-inch pot, or three in a twelve incher, but the soil must be especially well-draining. (Remember that *Lycoris* is native to the

The Spider Lily can almost bat its eyelashes.

quickly draining volcanic soil of the Japanese islands. This means you should mix half-and-half potting soil and sand.) At this point, your potted Lycoris bulbs can either go outside in the hot summer garden or stay inside in a sunny window.

Water the pot, but remember that *Lycoris* prefers things on the dry side. The soil should never be soggy. The flower stalk will appear sometime in late September or early October, pushing higher and higher like a flagpole until, one morning, it begins to unfurl its pinkish-red flowers.

Then you'll wonder how on earth you ever got along without this fabulous flower. It's guaranteed that even the crustiest Yankee will be amazed when this Spider Lily wakes up and bats her curled, eyelashlike stamens. While the plant is blooming, keep it watered and display it proudly. The pots look great on a patio or marching down the stairs, or make stunning table arrangements. Heck, take your Spider Lily to parties if you want to.

The sad thing about splendor is that it has to end sometime, and eventually your Spider Lily will fade. Because the bulbs are cheap (about fifty cents each), you can just toss everything away after the flower goes. But if you are thrifty, it is very simple to keep your Lycoris going year after year.

Lycoris's leaves will appear after the flower (sometime in late fall), and these must be kept safe from ex-treme cold temperatures. The easiest way to do this is to bring the pot inside and put it in a sunny window. Although the leaves are not as showy as the flower, they do have a beauty of their own. They grow to about eight inches long and have a pale stripe down the midrib. The foliage stays compact and looks a bit like a dainty spider plant, and, in fact, can be treated just like that easy-to-care-for houseplant—keep watered and fertilize sparingly.

The foliage stays nice and green indoors during winter and spring, and slowly begins to turn brown sometime around June. This is the signal that *Lycoris* is going to take a short nap before beginning her flowering cycle again. (It would have been during this dormant period that the supplier dug up the bulb to send it to you.) When all the leaves have turned brown, trim them away and put the pot outside in the sun. As before, keep the soil on the dryish side until, sometime around late September, Spider Lily gives a subterranean yawn and begins stretching up her flower stalks again.

Don't bother to brag to your North Carolinian garden friends about growing Spider Lily. They won't understand. But in the North, the little bit of attention you give to growing *Lycoris radiata* will be amply rewarded. Although Spider Lily is one of those who have always depended on the kindness of strangers, she sure is delightful to have around.

Melasphaerula: Iridaceae

❧

George Nicholson of the Royal Botanic Garden at Kew couldn't have been more enthusiastic about Fairy Bells. In the 1886 edition of *The Illustrated Dictionary of Gardening* he wrote that Melasphaerula is a "very pretty, greenhouse, bulbous plant with an elegant and graceful habit" and produces "a profusion of flowers which remain in perfection for a considerable time." Although Nicholson's intentions were obviously otherwise, his praise was the horticultural equivalent of the kiss of death, because shortly after, this plant nearly disappeared entirely from general cultivation.

The encouraging news is that every word, except one, Nicholson wrote about Fairy Bells is true—it is pretty, bulbous, elegant, graceful, and perfectly floriferous, but you do not need a greenhouse to grow this sweet old thing at home. As a fool-proof, inexpensive windowsill plant, Melasphaerula is perched on the brink of a comeback, and once you experience its ethereal, winter-time presence, you'll wonder how it was ever allowed to slip away. Fairy Bells—tiny, wispy, white flowers flittering by the score amongst grass-green foliage—is an old-time, gentle pleasure worth reviving in these modern, not-so-gentle times. We could all use a little magic right now.

Fairy Bells comes from places that sound imaginary; they are native to the Cape of Good Hope, Namaqualand, and Little Karoo. The Genus *Melasphaerula* is monotypic (this means that *ramosa* is the only species) and gets its name from *melas,* "black," and the diminutive of *sphaira,* "globe." The corms look like little black

The tiny corms of Melasphaerula are a cinch to force and produce delicate white flowers for almost six weeks.

marbles, and having been introduced in 1786, probably came to Europe by way of the Dutch East India Company garden located in Table Bay. Because Melasphaerula is a natural winter-flowerer found in bushy, shady places in the wild, it makes the perfect little corm for those whose indoor gardening equipment comes under the headings "Rudimentary" and "Zilch."

Growing instructions for *Melasphaerula* are very similar to those for its countryman *Chasmanthe*. The corms are available in late autumn and early winter and should be planted as soon as they arrive. Although some experts would shudder, put up to twenty-five corms in a pot that is about four inches deep and seven inches across. (Experts prefer to have fewer flowers in a pot, but Fairy Bells looks better with, and seems to enjoy, close company.) The corms should be covered with about one inch of soil, and the soil should contain enough sand to be quick-draining. Place the pot in a light window that does not get direct sun, and do not water at all until bright green tips of the leaves appear —anywhere from one week to a month later.

The foliage is soft, like grass, and a heart-stopping shade of pale green that instantly reminds one of the spring not so far off. Water sparingly, but don't let the soil get too dry. The leaves will grow and get fuller, and about six weeks after they first pop up, a threadlike flowering stem will appear. Then another and another and another will rise above the graceful grassy leaves until one day they begin to burst forth with flocks of half-inch-wide flowers of shimmering white. Each flower has six pointed petals, and each petal is minutely

Melasphaerula joins pots of emerging Roman Hyacinths and purple-leaved Oxalis on the author's dining-room table. Although the children must learn to balance dinner plates on their laps, they have an indoor garden all winter.

waved and marked with a streak of deep purple. As the stems are branched, each one produces up to ten iridescent flowers that swing around and through the foliage like little Peter Pans on wires. The flowers are very long-lasting, and as new stems keep appearing for at least a month, your Fairy Bells show will keep on going throughout the darkest days of winter.

After this long period of flowering, the leaves will begin to die back as *Melasphaerula* prepares for dormancy. This is the time to curtail watering and let the soil become completely dry. When all the leaves have withered, cut them off and turn the pot on its side as a signal that it should not be watered. Your Fairy Bells will sleep for the entire summer. Then, in late autumn, remember to peer into the sideways pot for signs that your plant is beginning to stir. When the first leaves appear, turn the pot upright, water, and let the the whole Fairy Bell show begin again.

And whatever you do, don't forget to show off your Melasphaerulas once they are in bloom. Remember that they were almost lost to cultivation, so play the part of a plant promoter. Tell everyone how pretty, rewarding, easy, and inexpensive (about ten dollars for twenty-five corms) they are. Unusual plants like this deserve our attention, and saving a plant like *Melasphaerula* is just about as easy as clapping your hands for Tinker Bell.

Muscari: Liliaceae

ﻬ

The mystery about muscaris is that they were among the most maligned bulbs. In *Dutch Bulbs and Gardens* (1909) author Una Silberrad makes the offhand remark that muscaris "are a good deal grown in Holland, and are coming into much favor in England, no one knows why." A decade later, an English garden encyclopedia lamanted: "It is strange that certain races of plants should be neglected in gardens although vigorous and beautiful in color. The muscaris are in this throng."

It is puzzling why grape hyacinths, which provide one of the best blues of spring, have gotten such short shrift for so long. But if Alice Morse Earle had had her way, *Muscari* would not have suffered this indignity for long.

Earle was a turn-of-the-century American garden writer who lived in Brooklyn, New York. Her passion (like that of many other horticultural writers of that time) was "old-fashioned" gardens and flowers. Her books—among them *Old Time Gardens* (1901) and *Sun Dials and Roses of Yesterday* (1902)—provide today's readers with invaluable firsthand information and photographs of American gardens of the nineteenth century, as well as an early and learned perspective on horticulture from the colonial period onward.

Alice Morse Earle loved grape hyacinths, and she made a point of noting that John Ruskin, the most widely read and influential English essayist of his time, shared her enthusiasm. She quoted his description of muscaris: "It was as if a cluster of grapes and a hive of honey had been distilled and pressed together into one small boss of celled and beaded blue."

Muscari armeniacum *has a sweet fragrance and matte-blue color that renders it indispensable for the spring garden.*

Besides their lovely color, muscaris also have a wonderful perfume that Louise Beebe Wilder, a contemporary of Miss Earle's, loved. (*Muscus* is Latin for "musk," and certain species carry this scent.) It has been described as "a mixture of the real old clove carnation and the ecclesiastical odor of night-scented stock." It was for this sweet scent that they were once called Baby's Breath, a name now almost entirely associated with the small white flowers of *Gypsophila paniculata*.

If you are a thrifty gardener, there's yet another reason to grow muscaris: their price. Grape Hyacinths (*Muscari armeniacum* specifically) have constantly remained one of the least expensive and most reliable bulbs around. Sixty years ago, the more common muscaris cost about six dollars per hundred, and today's price remains around thirty dollars per hundred. If you plant a hundred, chances are good that a hundred sweet-scented spires will bloom, and keep blooming for up to six weeks. Where else can you get such pleasure for thirty cents? In fact, it's about .00714 cents a day, so treat yourself.

The name Grape Hyacinth first applied to *M. botryoides* and refers to the grapelike cluster that characterizes many species in the Genus *muscari*. There are at least forty species, but the easiest to get and grow is *M. armeniacum,* which is also now known as Grape Hyacinth. (Therefore we have grape hyacinth as a general term and, here, Grape Hyacinth as a specific name for *Muscari armeniacum*—just when you thought you were getting the hang of all this nomenclature business.)

M. armeniacum was introduced to English gardens sometime around 1878 from Trebizond, a Turkish port

until you're sure that this time you have positively goofed up and killed them all. Then, with hope in your heart and the end of February on your calendar, pot up those neglected grape hyacinths (you can squeeze in as many as you like), water them well, and put the pots in your cool, dark basement. Eureka! In about ten days they will be sprouting and asking, "So what's your worry?" and will simply get on with making lots of pretty blue spikes just in time for Easter decorations. If only the rest of life were so simple.

Because Grape Hyacinths are so easy to grow, they can be used in a huge variety of ways. Elizabeth Lawrence wrote that "a few dozen bulbs of *M. armeniacum* soon made pools of blue along the driveway." Louise Beebe Wilder had a blue and gold carpet "woven of Grape Hyacinth 'Heavenly Blue' and the little wild yellow tulip *T. sylvestris* closely planted and, here and there among them, . . . tufts of baby Meadow Rue (*Thalictrum minor*)." Wilder also underplanted a "snow white *Magnolia stellata*" with blue muscaris so that it appeared her snowy white shrub cast deep blue shadows on the ground.

A simple, pleasing combination is old-fashioned primroses and Grape Hyacinths, and for Russell Page's own imaginary garden, this great designer specified a long archway of hazelnut trees underplanted with double mauve primroses, anemones, hellebores, and "as many dwarf daffodil and tulip species, scillas, muscari, chionodoxa, and other small bulbs as I can afford."

Because Grape Hyacinths are so reliable, they can be counted upon to perform within a formally laid-out garden. There is perhaps no more beautiful example of this than at the White House in Washington. During the

now called Trabzon, by the firm Barr & Sons of *Narcissus* fame. The flower stands about nine inches tall, and its leaves, which appear in autumn, are thin and about twelve inches long. *M. armeniacum* blooms in May and has been known to stay in flower as late as mid-June north of New York. It makes a long-lasting cut flower and is perfect with violets and Lily-of-the-valley in a tiny, sweetly perfumed Mother's Day arrangement. 'Blue Spike', a sport (or spontaneous mutation) with double blue flowers, is definitely worth avoiding. It is decidedly diseased-looking—instead of forming neat little blue beads, the inflorescence appears to be bubbling over itself.

Muscari armeniacum is so easy to force for indoor blooming that it's almost embarassing. After planting as many as you like outside, leave at least twenty for inside flowering. You can leave these bulbs in their bags in the refrigerator almost all winter—in other words,

The inexpensive, reliable **Muscari armeniacum** *behaves well in formal gardens, too. Here in a design by Lynden B. Miller for the Conservatory Garden in Central Park, New York City.*

Kennedy Administration, the White House Rose Garden was redesigned, the beds adjacent to the Oval Office were spruced up, and a more suitable arena for the outdoor ceremonies was created. Now in spring four large *Magnolia soulangiana* anchor the rectangular lawn. Two long beds with flowering crabtrees are filled with various flowering bulbs and edged with a low bright-green clipped hedge. Just inside the hedges is a densely planted band of bright blue muscaris. The muscaris are not visible when one first enters the garden, but upon approaching the beds to look at other more conspicu-ously displayed flowers, their brilliant color suddenly jumps out. To orchestrate a surprise in such a small garden is a touch of horticultural genius. The long-neglected little Grape Hyacinth, maligned no more, was finally given its due.

107

Narcissus: Amaryllidaceae

❧

N. BULBOCODIUM—HOOP PETTICOAT DAFFODIL · N. TAZETTA VAR. ORIENTALIS—CHINESE SACRED LILY · NARCISSUS 'KING ALFRED'

Although it is entirely possible to go nuts over *Narcissus,* it is really the genus's classification system that drives people cuckoo. Peter Barr, the King of Daffodils, wrote in 1884: "There is a tradition that Sweet, the botanist, went mad whilst trying to straighten out or unravel the knotted string which holds the whole bunch of these golden daffodils together."

The whole problem begins with the fact that daffodils, jonquils, and narcissuses are all kinds of *Narcissus.* While some (especially Southerners) insist that these names are distinct, others see them as interchangable pet names. At the turn of the century, "narcissus" and "daffodil" were synonymous, the first regarded as a Greek name (*narkoun,* "to benumb") and the second as English (probably from Old English *affodyle,* "early comer").

There are about seventy distinct *Narcissus* species and precisely infinity-zillion cultivars assigned to eleven divisions by the Royal Horticultural Society. There is also a modified version of the RHS's classification, but, frankly, either one makes about as much sense to the lay gardener as the old narcissus divisions called "Coffee Cup," "Tea Cup," and "Tea Saucer."

Evading the classification problem in this casual manner is bound to disturb some diehards, so for those that can't go a word further without studying it, please read all the fine print in *Hortus Third* and *The Classified List of Daffodil Names.* Just don't forget that Wordsworth's ten thousand daffodils left him prostrate and silly (". . . on my couch I lie . . . vacant or in a pensive mood . . ."). And whatever you do, don't forget poor Sweet, the botanist.

In Taoism the narcissus represents winter, but in other circles the daffodil was the flower of death. In "Lycidas," Milton placed "daffodillies" on the "laureate hearse," and in the South, old cemeteries sprout antique varieties of *Narcissus* for months on end. Although the exact symbolism has been lost, the narcissus-death connection can be traced all the way back to dried specimens of *Narcissus tazetta* on mummies' funeral wreaths from 1570 B.C.

But there are loads of fun reasons why people have grown anything and everything from the Genus *Narcissus* for centuries on end. The Big Three Plant Guys—Clusius, Gerard, and Parkinson—all wrote about *Narcissus.* Clusius traveled to Spain and wrote of six kinds he found there in *Rariorum aliquot stirpium per Hispanias . . .* (1576). Gerard grew twenty-four kinds of daffodils in 1597, and by 1627, Parkinson had more than eighty.

Parkinson probably acquired his many bulbs from sailors at the port of Bristol, which had a large Spanish and Portuguese trade during that time. (Bristol was also where Clusius went in search of *Iris xiphioides,* the Spanish native imported to Bristol in such quantity that it became known as English Iris.)

Horticultural historian Sir Sacheverell Sitwell (of the famously eccentric and aristocratic English family) points out that some of Parkinson's eighty daffodils suffered an unusual fate. Sitwell implies that it was typical of the plant-snobbish Parkinson to praise varieties that

The growing fields at Brent and Becky Heath's Daffodil Mart in Gloucester, Virginia, are heaven for the narcissus nut.

Old-fashioned Poet's Narcissus in a city garden.

were almost impossible for the ordinary gardener to obtain. No sooner did Parkinson brag about his daffodils—especially the yellow Hoop Petticoat, the Miniature Rush-leaved, the tiny *N. minimus,* and the Angel's Tears—than they vanished from the garden scene altogether. In fact, Parkinson's antique daffodils disappeared from cultivation for two centuries until nineteenth-century plantsman Peter Barr took upon himself an unusual mission: to travel to the Breton and Portuguese habitats of Parkinson's bulbs, collect them, and reintroduce them to general cultivation.

Peter Barr, the King of Daffodils, was nuts over *Narcissus.* A Scot with such a strong burr "that his own grandchildren could hardly understand him" he began his search for Parkinson's lost daffodils in 1887 (at age sixty-two), traveling to Portugal, Spain, and France. Even though he spoke no foreign language, and even

Nineteenth-century plant explorer Peter Barr tirelessly promoted the narcissus for outdoor . . .

. . . and indoor cultivation— these photographed in the pithouse at Stonecrop Nurseries, Cold Spring, New York.

though he had never ridden before, he went by mule and horse, carrying pictures of the plants he wanted to find. About 7,000 feet high in the Pyrenees, he found Parkinson's *N. moschatus,* which had disappeared about two and a half centuries earlier. He found other types, too, collecting a few thousand bulbs here, several thousand there, and a jillion somewhere else—in those days, a perfectly acceptable way to collect bulbs. (It would probably have been a waste of breath to talk to him about not collecting in the wild.)

After meeting this challenge, Barr embarked, at age seventy-seven, upon a five-year around-the-world daffodil-promoting trip. He traveled to Japan, China, Australia, New Zealand, islands in the Pacific, South Africa, and the United States.

But earlier, as a warm-up for his first big trip, Barr wrote a book on his favorite subject, *Ye Narcissus or Daffodil Flower* (1884), promoting both outdoor and indoor cultivation: "The narcissus . . . like many another neglected flower, is now reasserting its position, and claiming its proper place in the general economy of border decoration and as a cut flower for furnishing vases." Barr was also the founder of the famous Barr & Sons bulb nurseries in Surrey, England.

Following the King's advice, one should consider daffodils both for gardens and for forcing. Outside, the daff will bloom year after year undisturbed by disease or critters (their bulbs are poisonous), and inside, one can follow the great Victorian tradition of forcing.

To begin with, the most un-daffodilly-looking narcissus (and perhaps the trickiest of these three to grow)

Today there is little danger of the daffodil disappearing from sight. This naturalized collection grows in Suzanne Bales's New York garden.

The Victorians were crazy about **N. tazetta** *var.* **orientalis** *(Chinese Sacred Lily), an easy-to-force, sweetly scented narcissus with* **beaucoup** *blossoms. These were forced by Peggy Newcomb at Monticello and shipped overnight to her grateful friends in New York.*

Narcissus bulbocodium var. conspicuus, *pictured here at the Daffodil Mart in Virginia, is an unusual bulb for the Southern garden.*

is the Hoop Petticoat. *N. bulbocodium* was one of Parkinson's daffodils that had been lost to general cultivation until Barr rediscovered it. The Bulbocodium is a curious species of flowers with very thin leaves and flowers with almost no perianth segments. They have very wide mouths that are pulled in a bit around the rim like an old-fashioned crinoline. Another old name for this flower is Medusa's Trumpet, and the thin perianth segments do look a bit like snakes sticking out from behind a big brassy horn.

There are several Bulbocodiums, but the easiest is var. *conspicuus,* which passersby can see naturalized throughout the waterside fields at the Daffodil Mart in Virginia. Zone 7 is generally considered their northernmost hardiness zone. A garden writer from central Ontario (zone 4!) claims to keep a few coming back each year, but it seems a shame to put such a sweet little plant at risk.

In cold climates these pure yellow Hoop Petticoats are wonderful for forcing. Put six to eight in a pot and place in a cool (not freezing) spot until the roots are full. Move to a warmer (50 to 60 degrees) north-facing window, or another position that does not receive direct sunlight or high temperatures. Pots of *N. bulbocodium* look like a collection of yellow petticoats billowing in the breeze. Although the unbiquious Paperwhite had been around for ages (in this country over 200 years),

Narcissus bulbocodium was favored by Victorians as their favorite narcissus for forcing—until a new fad hit during the last decade of their century.

The Victorians went wild over forcing the Chinese Sacred Lily, which in the search for accurately named flowers gets zero points. It is not Chinese, it was not considered sacred, and it is not a lily. But it scores high in other areas: *Narcissus tazetta* var. *orientalis* is deliciously fragrant. It produces an unbelievable number of cream and golden-yellow flowers. It is easy—the bulb blooms six to eight weeks after potting and requires no elaborate cooling. In short, to know it is to love it.

Dioscorides wrote about both *N. tazetta* (the main type of which the Sacred Lily is a variety) and *N. poeticus* in *De Materia Medica* of the first century A.D. Tazettas are from southern Europe and western Asia, but traveled to northern India, China, and Japan at an early date along the old trade routes, and from there made the jump back to European gardens. Both singles and doubles were in Britain by 1597, and it is these old cluster types—'Star', 'Christmas', 'Pearl', 'Gold Dollars', and others—that are so beloved in Southern gardens.

The Chinese Sacred Lily is the tazetta the Victorians took straight to their hearts. It was sometimes called the Joss Lily or Lien Chu Lily, and although this flower was popular in China as a New Year's decoration (a version of Paperwhites for Christmas), these exotic names were promoted as advertising gimmicks to make the flowers seem more valuable.

Besides it wonderful fragrance and pretty golden cups (*tazza* means "cup"), the Chinese Sacred Lily has an

flowering season. It is also fun to water-force the Chinese Sacred Lily, as the Victorians often did.

In a pretty, shallow bowl, arrange about an inch of gravel, and place bulbs on top of this so that they nearly touch each other. Fill in with gravel around the bulbs so they don't move about. (Use pretty rocks, please.) Fill the bowl with water until it nearly—but not quite—touches the bulbs, and place it in a cool (45 to 50 degrees) dark closet to root.

Some people put charcoal in the water in hopes of keeping it fresh, but, truly, there is only one way to keep it from getting murky and smelly. About twice a week, take your bulb bowls to the kitchen sink and gently fill the bowl with lukewarm water until it runs out the top. This replaces the old water with fresh. Then, holding everything in place (this might take four hands), tilt the bowl and pour the water out until it reaches its former just-below-the-bulbs level.

When the roots are curling around the bowl and there is about one inch of growth on top (the number of weeks for this stage varies widely so keep checking), bring the bowl into a light, cool (around 50 degrees) spot until the buds are well developed. Then, when the flowers are ready to open, about six to eight weeks after starting, place your Chinese Sacred Lilies wherever the whim carries you. They are certainly special enough to decorate the parlor or will make the most wonderful winter bouquet you could ever give.

Several old books cite a method of forcing even greater numbers of Chinese Sacred Lily blooms. It sounds a bit drastic, but is certainly worth trying. With

abundant crop of flowers. Although one writer's claim of ninety-seven flowers from a single bulb is hard to believe, one bulb does reliably produce several scapes, and it isn't uncommon to have twelve flowers dangling from a single scape. For outdoor growing, this is undoubtedly a bulb for warm climates, Southern California probably being the perfect spot. All the rest of us can force the Chinese Sacred Lily in pots, with the leaves left to ripen and build up the bulb for the next a very sharp knife or scalpel, make an incision crosswise jut through the outer skin of the bulb, about one inch from the top. Repeat on the other side, taking care not to cut more than the top layer or to injure the bulb. These cuts apparently allow additional leaves and flowers to pop from the bulb, sometimes allowing up to twelve spikes of bloom from a single water-forced Sacred Lily (and might account for a claim of ninety-seven flowers from a solitary bulb).

After such a demanding performance, the water-forced, spent bulb deserves a decent burial in your compost pile, perhaps with a few lines from Keats: "A thing of beauty is a joy for ever . . . and such are Daffodils/ With the green world they live in."

The third daffodil suitable for either outside or indoors is the robust, handsome 'King Alfred', who was once an expensive treat but now has been relegated to the "that old thing' list. In fact, there have been rumors that 'King Alfred' is no longer actually sold, and that impostor cultivars are placed in your parcel when you ask for him. It's time for everyone to remember Peter Barr's hard work and make sure that this classic yellow trumpet, who appeared in 1899, is not allowed to vanish from our garden scenes.

For many years 'King Alfred' was the standard for yellow trumpet daffodils. He blooms early, is very hardy, and unlike some daffodils does not easily succumb to rot. He is the first-generation offspring of Clusius's *N. hispanicus,* and with his twisted blue-green foliage, large waved perianth, and flanged trumpet, "Freddy" is very much the son of his regal Spanish father.

Narcissus 'King Alfred' mingles with wild blue Quaker Ladies in a late springtime arrangement.

A catalogue from 1914 lists 'King Alfred' for a princely fifteen dollars per bulb, noting that he is "strong, vigorous, and healthy . . . a superb variety for exhibition, pot, and border culture." The Royal Horticulture Society gave him a First Class Certificate, and he won the Premier Prize from the Midland Daffodil Society.

'King Alfred' is now one of the least expensive daffodils and remains one of the most reliable. In a mixed collection of bulbs for naturalizing, 'King Alfred' will appear year after year, like an old general, with medals proudly pinned on, preening at the Veterans Day parade. He's big, he's bold, and he's beautiful. Don't let the others put you off just because he's older.

As an early bloomer outdoors, 'King Alfred' is also easy to force in pots or boxes. Plant bulbs as early as possible and keep outside in the cold, but protected from extreme temperature, for at least two months.

Move to a cool, dark place to stimulate further root growth and, when the tops appear, bring into indirect light. Too much warmth, especially at first, will induce overly long, limp leaves and may cause the buds to "blast" or shrivel without opening. Keep springtime temperatures in mind—usually it's still sweater weather —and keep your forced plants near a window or in another scenic but chilly spot.

Depending on where your garden is, you can grow all three of these old *Narcissus* outside or indoors. The bulbs should be planted as early in autumn as possible. However, as with anything else, just try to get to it as soon as you can. Timing is important, but to procrastinators who cannot do *anything* on time, it should be mentioned that one of the cheeriest woodland groupings of daffodils in Garrison, New York, was planted years ago using the highly unorthodox Galligan method.

Although most gardeners plant spring-blooming bulbs during the golden days of autumn . . .

. . . these flowers were picked from bulbs planted under chunks of ice in the dead of winter. From the Galligan garden in Garrison, New York.

Paperwhite Narcissuses, yellow tulip petals, and purple Crocus speciosus were air-dried in baskets near the fire or hung upside down in the pantry.

The Galligan method is absolutely unapproved by any expert, but often employed by amateur gardeners. Long after winter arrives and the ground has frozen solid, locate the boxes of bulbs you have placed in the garage along with the other things you needed to finish up in the garden. Then, deciding where you want to plant your bulbs, use a crowbar to level up a hunk of frozen earth—much as roadworkers lift large manhole covers. Place bulbs in the exposed soil, make a pretty speech acknowledging their patience, and replace the solid chunk of earth gently on top. Repeat until all your bulbs are planted. Not every single bulb will bloom,

Grow enough Narcissuses to send to your friends. Pluck them while still in bud, wrap carefully in plastic, and ship overnight delivery.

118

but a large percentage will, and this method certainly produces more flowers than just leaving the bulbs in the garage until you clean it out in 1998.

Whether you force your daffs or grow them outside, it is easy to prolong your enjoyment by drying their flowers. Cut the daffodils off the stems and either air-dry them in baskets or gently cover them in a mixture of one-half cornmeal and one-half laundry borax. It's quick and easy, and a colorful mixture looks pretty in little dishes. Just keep those annoying potpourri squeezers from rustling through your mixtures and spoiling their delicate forms.

But the most delicious pleasure of all to be had from daffodils is to send them to a friend by overnight delivery. This was a speciality of Peter Barr, Daffodil King, back in the day when the post went overnight. His advice was: "If you post flowers to your friends, pack them in the bud stage. . . . They pack readily . . . and much more safely than if further advanced. . . . Flower buds cut in this way open out fresher and attain a larger size than they would have had they remained uncut. . . . You may send fifty or sixty Daff buds in a comparatively small box." Today, you can wrap wet paper towels around the cut end of the stems and put flowers and all into a plastic bag. Blow the bag up to cushion the flowers and place this into an overnight-delivery box. Your flowers will arrive fresh, uncrushed, and far nicer than anything from Teleflora. You might include a small card in the box with the words of Mohomet: "He that has two cakes of bread, let him sell one of them for some flowers of the narcissus, for bread is food for the body, but narcissus is the food of the soul." For the less sentimental, you could say, "Nuts over narcissus and crazy about you."

Oxalis: Oxalidaceae

O. VERSICOLOR

Many people have early memories involving the Oxalis Family. All children are warned *not* to eat the ubiquitous Wood Sorrel—the small plant that has bright-green, shamrocklike leaves—yet every child since Adam and Eve's has nibbled those forbidden, weird-tasting greens. Different names and different folk tales are bound to occur wherever Wood Sorrel does, but in the Blue Ridge Mountains of southern Virginia, children chew the vinegary leaves when they're thirsty and don't want to go all the way back home for a drink of water. This knowledge gets passed down as the older children always demonstrate this survival tactic for the benefit of the younger ones, and swear that it's an old Indian trick, and that "if you tell Mom she'll wallop us.' Eating Wood Sorrel, like other mysteries in life, is just another one of those things you can't discuss with your parents.

The Genus *Oxalis* is very large and gets its name from that taste children find so undeniably good (*oxys,* "sharp," and *als,* "salt"). Although there are a few temperate-zone oxalises, most of the species are tropical. Many are harmful if eaten in large quantities (your parents were right after all), but one species, Oca (*Oxalis tuberosa*), is an important food in Peru. If you want to keep your children from nibbling their local Wood Sorrel, just tell them that some natives use members of this genus as a medicine to help expel tapeworms. That should do the trick.

Another arcane use for oxalis is that, supposedly, the crushed leaves can be used to remove inkstains, but putting aside all these really useful ideas, just grow this pretty plant as a cheery, winter-blooming houseplant because it has one really neat party trick.

Oxalis versicolor is a classic member of the genus, having been introduced from South Africa in 1774. The Victorians were keen for it as a houseplant, but found that it needed a lot of sun to bloom. For this reason, it became a particularly popular plant in the South. But today, when heavy drapes and lace curtains aren't as prevalent as they were in our great-grandmothers' time, most houses and apartments have plenty of light to unfold the peppermint-stick-striped buds of this charming little pet.

Oxalis versicolor tubers can be purchased in autumn and winter, and, as it is a compact plant, can be planted in a rather small pot. Pack them in, but just barely cover with a fine sandy grit. Water once, do not water again until the leaves appear, then give enough water to keep leaves pert. The leaflets, which are skinnier than the usual shamrock shape, will create a soft green mound, and within a month, tiny creamy flowers rimmed in pink will appear.

The flowers possess a magic that will entrance you. At night they are furled exactly like a parasol, but as soon as the sunlight touches them, the tiny buds slowly unfold right before your eyes. The effect of a whole pot of *Oxalis versicolor* opening up is like watching an entire street of Victorian ladies elegantly unfurling parasol after parasol in an elaborate, sun-shading ritual. It might be just you, a bowl of Wheaties, and a cup of coffee watching, but *Oxalis versicolor* will happily perform this

A wintertime tabletop of
Oxalis versicolor *grown by*
Peggy Newcomb.

trick day after day as the winter sun moves across the breakfast table. There couldn't be a more festive way to start a winter day.

Oxalis versicolor will stay in flower for about six weeks. When it dies back, let the pot get bone-dry and leave it tipped on its side for the summer. When the leaves begin to poke up late next autumn, you can start the whole process over again. By then your children will have had their fill of the outdoor Wood Sorrel, so you won't have to worry about them surreptitously munching on your indoor kind. Besides, if one of them accidentally gets ink on the couch, you can pick a few oxalis leaves and try an old Indian trick of your own.

Puschkinia: Liliaceae

P. SCILLOIDES—STRIPED SQUILL

The tiny Striped Squill, which Louise Beebe Wilder called "a pretty trinket of spring," is, for all intents and purposes, an only child. The puschkinia has many, many cousins because it comes from one of the largest families of flowering plants, but although *Liliaceae* has 250 genera and more than 3,500 species, *Puschkinia* itself is a very small genus. It seldom boasts more than one species in catalogues, *Hortus Third,* or other references.

This flower was named for Count Apollo Apollovich Mussin-Pushkin (or Pouschkin), a Russian botanist who collected throughout the Caucasus. Introduced in 1805, this little guy was first indentified as *Adamsia scilloides,* and has also been called *Scilla sicula, Puschkinia hyacinthoides,* and *P. sicula.* The synonyn *P. libanotica* still occasionally pops up, so be on the lookout for it in catalogues.

Striped Squill is related to the true scillas and to Glory-of-the-snow (*Chiondoxa*), but the most useful piece of information one can know about *Puschkinia scilloides* is that it grows wild at elevations sometimes over 10,000 feet. Having no fear of frozen ground, it flourishes near the forever replenished edge of melting snow anywhere from Lebanon to Afganistan, easily surviving minus 30 degrees Fahrenheit. Puschkinia is one of the true hardy boys in the bulb department, and a welcome sight when it seems that spring will never arrive.

Puschkinia may not, in fact, be an only child, but one with a mysterious sibling. *Hortus Third* mentions, but does not list, a second species, but E. A. Bowles, that gentleman gardener and bulb expert, did not believe that one existed at all. Of *P. libanotica,* the "other" puschkinia, Bowles wrote: "If you buy what is offered as *P. libanotica,* you will get *scilloides,* for they are but one and the same, though often listed as distinct, and sometimes you are invited to pay more for the other, so always buy the cheaper." At today's price of twelve dollars per hundred, you are not going to find anything much cheaper, anyway.

Puschkinia figured in the great garden friendship between Elizabeth Lawrence in North Carolina and Carl Krippendorf in Ohio. Correspondence between gardeners ("Mine blooms now," "Mine are over") has gone on for centuries. When exchanged with a beloved gardening friend, each season's achievements seem as fresh and absorbing as talk of baby steps and first words between doting parents.

In the preface to *The Little Bulbs: A Tale of Two Gardens,* Miss Lawrence wrote: "This is a tale of two gardens: mine and Mr. Krippendorf's. Mine is a small city back yard laid out in flower beds and gravel walks, with scraps of pine woods in the background; Mr. Krippendorf's is hundreds of acres of virgin forest." Who knows what delightful plant first brought these two together, but puschkinia gave them something to write about during the quiet season when many gardens are just mud and snow.

A mid-April 1947 letter from Mr. Krippendorf's Lob's Wood address reads: "The thermometer is thirty degrees on the front porch . . . and while I was out I found . . . a puschkinia, the first in several years. I planted some of these before 1914, and they disap-

Hardy Puschkinias bloom during such cold weather that it is probably best to dig some up for inside enjoyment. After flowering, these were put back in the garden and suffered no ill effects.

Puschkinias make a worthy gift to someone who will appreciate their delicate markings and sweet perfume.

peared. But I keep finding just a few, far from the original planting." In turn, Miss Lawrence noted that her puschkinias bloomed as early as February 9 in her North Carolina garden.

Ants are the reason for Mr. Krippendorf's wandering puschkinias. The surface of each seed has a kind of fatty oil the ants find particularly delectable. Just as they do with colchicums, the hungry ants schlep the seeds back to their nests, lick off the yummy oil, and then tidily discard the undamaged seed outside their homes. These industrious little creatures are quite happy to go a long way for puschkinia fat, so seeds may end up traveling from one end of the garden to the other. Perhaps puschkinias and colchicums are plants for gardeners who like surprises and aren't too worried about finding socks in their underwear drawer and vice versa.

Gardeners throughout the years have found puschkinias delightful. William Robinson found it "one of the most beautiful bulbous flowers," but its subtle charm deserves close observation. The leaves grow to only six inches, and the pale blue flowers are usually just half an inch long, and not more than an inch in diameter. The flower color is a very pale blue, decribed by Mrs. Wilder as "the color of skimmed milk," but each segment has a deeper blue line down the middle. Bowles said that the color reminded him of "the ghost of a scilla come back to earth." The puschkinia also has a sweet spicy perfume worth getting down on hands and knees to sniff.

Puschkinias are an easy treat. They look pretty in short grass under deciduous shrubs and trees and they are also fine for the rock garden. And, with help from the ants they will self-seed and naturalize, so they may pop up in some delightful new locations, too. Plant them in autumn and they will bloom in early spring outside, or they can be forced to bloom indoors, making tiny bouquets of ghostly-pale winter flowers.

Wherever you plant them, remember that puschkinias are quiet little cold-lovers; to be fully enjoyed, they should be close at hand. Mrs. Wilder wrote: "Do what you will with this little flower, it cannot be made a showy garden ornament. Spread it in hundreds, or gather it in close colonies on some sunny ledge in the rock garden, and it remains its gentle unobtrusive self. It is a flower meant for minute scrutiny, to hold in the hand or to bend over attentively, when its modest charms will be made plain to you." This, perhaps, makes puschkinias the perfect flowers to trade and discuss with your favorite garden friend.

Scilla: Liliaceae

S. SIBIRICA—SIBERIAN SQUILL

he Siberian Squill is a blue mystery. Other scillas were favored plants as early as the first part of the seventeenth century, but although the Siberian species was known in Europe at that time, this beautiful little flower was not officially introduced until almost two centuries later.

There is no mention of any particular person connected with this plant, no medicinal use, no classical reference, no interesting gossip at all except that *Hortus Third* and John Bryan spell the name "siberica" while everyone else spells is "sibirica." Surprisingly, "sibirica" is correct. Perhaps *S. sibirica* is the little squill that came in from the cold and has just been content to lead a quiet existence, or another possible explanation is that it was so small it just escaped everyone's notice. Sometimes small yet very beautiful plants (muscaris and puschkinias, for example) don't attract the fans that bigger plants do, but the garden would be awfully boring with only towering sunflower types in it.

Yet shortness doesn't really explain why *S. sibirica* ("to six inches") was ignored while *S. bifolia* ("to six inches") and *S. amoena* ("to six inches") were in cultivation in the early 1600s. Maybe the spy theory is the answer after all.

Scilla is a genus of eighty to ninety species, most native to Africa, Europe, and Asia. The name derives from *skullo*, "injure"; the bulbs are said to be very poisonous. The genus formerly included the bluebells so beloved in England, but these have changed their name and are now called *Endymion*.

One of the squills that attracted early attention was the former *S. alba*, the Sea Onion (now another name-changer, called *S. verna*). This one was "hung in the roof of the house to keep away witches and spirits" and may at one time have been mistakenly allied with the anti-witch alliums, all of which are edible. Sea Onion was also prescribed, presumably in small doses, for treatment of asthma and dropsy. Parkinson, Galen, and Pliny all wrote about it, and Clusius was prepared to go the final research mile and ingest what was called *Scilla*

Tiny blue Scillas at the Daffodil Mart, Gloucester, Virginia.

A carpet of sapphire-blue
Scillas at the Hunnewell
Estate in Boston,
Massachusetts.

Scillas, like Puschkinias, may be dug up for indoor enjoyment and later replanted in the garden for subsequent years of bloom.

rubra (probably *S. bifolia* 'Rosea') but was deterred by horrified Spaniards, who warned him that it was a very powerful poison.

In *Dutch Bulbs and Gardens,* the turn-of-the-century authors Una Silberrad and Sophie Lyall wrote: "One of the most beautiful of the early spring flowers is one practically without history, the *Scilla sibirica.* It is comparatively a newcomer in Dutch bulb fields for it was brought to Europe from Asia Minor, the Happy Land of bulb collectors, around 1800."

Twentieth-century plant historian Alice Coats pinpoints that *S. sibirica* was known on the continent before 1622, but it is generally agreed that it was not formally introduced until 1796. Miss Coats further reports that it was at first regarded as a tender plant that required winter protection—quite an odd notion to have been attached to a bulb from Siberia.

S. sibirica, in fact, seems to thrive without care, and true to its origins, will withstand winters that might send other less brave bulbs scurrying. Celia Thaxter grew *S. sibirica* in her island garden ten miles off the coast of New Hampshire, in the Isles of Shoals. Her father served as lighthouse keeper there, and after her marriage, Mrs. Thaxter spent summers there, keeping a small but beautiful garden. The tiny garden became famous, a floral magnet for visiting writers such as Sarah Orne Jewett and John Greenleaf Whittier, and, in 1894, Celia Thaxter—herself an accomplished writer—published her garden journal with illustrations by her friend Childe Hassam.

As Thaxter records in *An Island Garden,* each April 1, she would leave her winter home on the mainland for her island and her garden. "A small steam tug, the *Pinafore,* carries me and my household belongings over to the islands," she wrote, "and a pretty sight is the little vessel when she starts out from the old brown wharves and steams away down the Piscataqua River, with her hurricane deck awave with green leaves and flowers, for all the world like a May Day procession."

The green leaves and flowers that Thaxter took with her to the island garden were annuals she had started from seed during the winter in her mainland home. Some were germinated and raised to babyhood in eggshells, much as gardeners today use plantable peat pots. Thaxter gently cracked the shells right before placing them and their contents into the earth, thus allowing the delicate roots to emerge undisturbed.

Upon arriving at her island with her fragile cargo, Thaxter was greeted by hardy plants that had overwintered on the deserted, frozen island. Imagine the delight of being greeted by "the beauty of the pure white snowdrops," the "long, lovely bubbles of gold" crocuses, and "the little *Scilla sibirica* [that] hangs its enchanting bells out to the breeze, blue, oh, blue as the deep sea water at its bluest under cloudless skies."

'Spring Beauty' is the Siberian Squill most often offered now, and this is the one Miss Lawrence liked so much. At one time it was called *S. sibirica* var. *atroco-erula*, but 'Spring Beauty' seems now to be the name of choice in books and catalogues. This variety has flowers that last a remarkably long time and are a deep, deep blue. This little plant is surely a beauty, but otherwise its name is misleading: this flower actually arrives *before* spring does, but no one wants to be called 'Tail End of Winter Beauty'.

As Ceila Thaxter would agree, Siberian Squills are of the easiest culture, though they do require a cold period. They can be forced and, unlike many bulbs, will thrive outdoors the very next season if they are permitted to go through their leaf and dormant stages. If your garden is very, very cold when your squills bloom and it's too bitter to get out to visit them, you can dig up a small clump for indoor enjoyment. After their long blooming period, put the whole piece of turf back in the ground, protect it from getting zapped by any extraordinarily cold temperatures, and this same clump will bloom the following year.

Described as "bluer than anything else that grows," this little blue mystery, as another gardener says, "should always be on the shopping list." At less than twenty-four dollars per hundred, truer, bluer words were never written.

Sternbergia: Amaryllidaceae

S. CLUSIANA · S. LUTEA

Sternbergia has had the worst luck with misleading nicknames. Parkinson probably started the whole thing when he mistakenly decided to call one of them *Narcissus autumnalis major*. From this it is easy to see why someone anglicized the name to Autumn Daffodil and then, exaggerating a bit to make it even more exciting, Winter Daffodil.

Although members of *Amaryllidaceae*, sometimes called the Daffodil Family, sternbergias don't look like daffodils at all. Others have also dipped into the family name and called them "Yellow Amaryllis." Playing it safe, Thomas Jefferson's family friend Lady Skipwith referred to her sternbergias as "Yellow Autumn Amaryllis Daffodils." Nearby, in Colonial Williamsburg, they were sometimes called Autumn Crocus (another entirely different plant), and elsewhere they have been called "Mount Etna Lily" or even "Lily-of-the-field." But they are not daffodils, amaryllises, amaryllis-daffodils, crocuses, or lilies—they are sternbergias. It is not the world's most glamorous name, but it is the most accurate, and these cheerful autumn-blooming bulbs have enough going for them to deserve a name of their own.

The genus is small, with about five species. Three are fall-blooming, two flower in spring, and all are yellow except for the white *candida*. They were named after Count Caspar Sternberg, a prominent German botanist (1761–1838). Since they were known to gardeners long before Sternberg's birth, this may explain why they suffered such an identity crisis for so long. Imagine the confusion of being around for several centuries before the person you were named for was born.

Sternbergias are one of the bright notes of autumn and are especially popular in Southern gardens. But for quite a while they suffered the reputation of being sulky, temperamental bloomers that were likely to skip the autumnal dinner party even though the place cards had already been ordered. This reputation is unjust.

English garden writer Beverley Nichols had gardened for twenty years and written many books by the time he received a flash of sternbergia wisdom that changed his life. "I had known the sternbergia for many years and had grown it with varying success. Very varying," he wrote. But during a visit to Corfu, Nichols observed these plants in the wild, tumbling down a hillside, and after experiencing a Wordsworthian moment of enchantment, suddenly had a stroke of genius concerning their fickleness: ". . . a good honest word that I muttered to myself as I stood there on that little hill—the word drainage. That was the heart of the matter—drainage. It stood out a mile. For the sternbergias, as they cascaded over the rocks, were bold and brilliant. But as the slope became less steep they began to fade away."

Beverley Nichols's wit and wisdom were a delightful addition to garden writing at a time when Katharine S. White, Elizabeth Lawrence, Vita Sackville-West, Louise Beebe Wilder and E. A. Bowles were all busy elevating this genre beyond the how-to shelf. It was a lively period in garden literature, and Nichols's books, often illustrated by artists such as William McLaren and Rex Whistler, remain among the best. (Here are his sentiments about another bulb: "If you want snowdrops for

An unidentified sternbergia blooms next to the red stems of Poke (Phytolacca americana) at the Hunt Arboretum in North Carolina.

Autumn borders of
Sternbergia clusiana *and*
blue Caryopteris at
Longwood Gardens in
Kennett Square,
Pennsylvania.

massing under trees, there are all sorts of cheap varieties. However, they are at least six weeks later than the
elwesii, and I myself will have none of them. I shall
probably go bankrupt, with my tastes. But I would
rather be made bankrupt by a bulb merchant than by a
chorus girl.")

But to return to the presumed fickleness of sternbergias, Nichols was absolutely right when he deduced the
importance of drainage: they work best on the tops or
sides of slopes or in gravelly soil. Other gardeners have
grappled with sternbergia challenges, either real or ru-
mored, among them the supposition that they could not
survive a cold snap. Yet a turn-of-the-century bulb catalogue lists *S. lutea* as "hardy" ("Henderson's Bulb Culture," 1904), and Elizabeth Lawrence wrote that one of
her friends reported them surviving 15 degrees below
zero, and, further, that *S. lutea* grew and bloomed out-

A closeup of the **S. clusiana** *at Longwood shows that, unlike* **S. lutea**, *the flowers appear without foliage.*

doors at the Gardiner Museum in Boston, a climate that certainly gets its share of cold weather. Louise Beebe Wilder, too, could claim firsthand knowledge of their hardiness in her garden fifty miles north of New York City. *S. lutea*, she wrote, was "given a reputation for tenderness which is quite undeserved. It has grown in this cold garden for many years, even withstanding the record winter of 1933–34 without injury." She planted her bulbs in August "on a sunny slope of the rock garden in well-drained rather stony soil and they have done well and multiplied. . . . My bulbs are given a warm rock at their back, on the north side which insures them the summer baking which seems to be required if they are to flower freely. . . . In my climate the leaves last over winter, appearing still richly green when we take off the blanket of salt hay in early spring. . . ."

"Bloom is more a matter of lime than latitude . . ." is Elizabeth Lawrence's summation of the cold-hardiness debate. Perhaps sternbergias had occasionally dropped out of the dinner party because they got tired of bad seating arrangements and improper diet. Remember drainage, add small quantities of lime to your beds, and your sternbergia success may surprise all the nay-sayers of the garden world.

One stern word of caution about sternbergias is that they are on the notorious list for wild collection. Because they are native to the Middle East, where many bulb species have been collected to the point of near extinction, it is best to ask your supplier where his bulbs were raised. One of the safer sources for these bulbs is Dutch growers. This bulb was once very popular in the gardens of Virginia, and Elizabeth Lawrence reported in 1942 that the bulb's revived popularity was due to renewed distribution from these old Southern sources. Once again, ask your supplier.

There are at least two spring-flowering sternbergias, but spring is a season when so much else is going on that it seems best to save your sternbergia budget for the more unusual autumn-flowering species. The two that are the easiest to come by are *S. Clusiana* (about twelve dollars a bulb) and *S. lutea* (about fourteen dollars a dozen).

S. clusiana was, of course, named for that early bulb fancier Clusius, but these little guys appeared on the scene rather late—at least one source says as late as 1825. An old synonym is *S. macrantha,* which refers to this bulb's large flowers (*macranthus* means "large-flowered"). There is little or no stem and the foliage dies away before the flowers appear, so *S. clusiana* in bloom looks like a bare golden flame rising from the earth.

S. clusiana is native to Turkey and Syria and is probably a bit more tender than *S. lutea.* The foliage must be able to develop in early spring, so if your garden is prone to late heavy frost, it might be an idea to grow

S. lutea *in the October woods*
134 *at the Hunt Arboretum.*

❧

Sternbergia lutea *(and a stray cyclamen) in the woodland collection of William Lanier Hunt in North Carolina.*

your *S. clusiana* in pots that can be sheltered from extreme cold.

At Longwood Gardens in Pennsylvania there is an outstanding fall display of *Sternbergia clusiana* that's worth traveling to see. Located thirty miles west of Philadelphia, the property was originally owned by William Penn. In 1700 it was sold to the Peirce family —fellow Quakers who shared a deep respect for nature and an ardent curiosity about plants. The family began a small arboretum that later attracted the fabulously wealthy Pierre du Pont to the property. He bought it in 1906 and began developing a garden there that has been described as "the ultimate expression of an estate garden of the 1920s."

Longwood is spectacular at all seasons, but for those who seek a quiet autumn thrill, there is double border of *Sternbergia clusiana* planted under *Caryopteris clandonensis* that looks like a long row of birthday candles producing clouds of blue smoke. This is an idea certainly worth trying at home, even if on a smaller scale.

The other fall-blooming sternbergia to try is *S. lutea,* a native of southeastern Europe, Palestine, and Persia. Because of its homeland, this is another flower that may have been one of the "lilies of the field of the Bible. (It seems that *all* the flowers native to this part of the world are may-have-been-lilies-of-the-field.) This sternbergia, Parkinson's "Autumn Daffodil," was in cultivation by 1596, and is the one to try—following Mrs. Wilder's earlier recommendations—if your winters are cold.

Sternbergia lutea will bloom the first season, even when planted as late as September. The leaves peek up first (eventually growing eight inches long) and the bright yellow, crocuslike flowers appear soon after. In a dry, sunny spot—such as on a hillside—they will colonize nicely.

For any devoted garden traveler, there is an extraordinary naturalized patch of *Sternbergia lutea* at the Hunt Arboretum in Chapel Hill, North Carolina. William Lanier Hunt planted them twenty-five years ago in what is now 600 acres of protected woodland, a green island in the midst of sprawling urbanization. Hunt, now a lively octogenarian, has multiple claims to gardening fame: he was a close friend of Elizabeth Lawrence's, he has written a weekly garden column since 1929, he helped start the Southern Garden History Society, his woodland garden has a marvelous patch of cyclamen raised from seeds from the great E. A. Bowles's garden, and it was he who inspired Nancy Goodwin at Montrose Nursery to raise cyclamen from seed for the American market.

Mr. Hunt has dedicated his life to matters horticultural, and he delights in giving personal tours of the Hunt Arboretum, wearing out garden visitors half his age. He scampers over the wooded hillside that glows with sternbergias in October, pointing out companion plantings of *Solidago caesia,* the Blue-stemmed Goldenrod, and Irish Ivy. He loves his sternbergias, and as he throws himself onto the ground in the middle of hundreds of their golden cups, he smiles winningly and proclaims: "They are so vain!"

Tulipa: Liliaceae

ᔰ

T. CLUSIANA—LADY TULIP, CANDY TULIP · T. TARDA

T. SAXATILIS

*I*f there is anything worse than going over old ground, it has to be going over and over and over old ground. What you don't know about the Dutch tulipomania of 1634–37 you are not going to read here. As Buckner Hollingsworth wearily noted in *Flower Chronicles*, "the part played by the tulip in high finance is almost too well known to bear repeating." Tulips were the junk bonds of another era. Having read the once-interesting stories about 'Semper Augustus' for the tenth time, no one would blame you for deciding there is not much else besides tulipomania to read about tulips. But you would be wrong.

Don't look for tulip references in the usual old places. They don't appear in mythology, they were not used medicinally, and although tulips are native to parts of the world that have been civilized forever, these showy flowers somehow manage not to appear in classical literature. And, as Sir Daniel Hall, an authority on the tulip, wrote, it is "somewhat remarkable that neither Theophrastus, Dioscorides, nor Pliny should have noticed so conspicuous a plant of which several are not uncommon in Greece and Ionia." It seems odder still that there were no tulips in Italian paintings until the mid-sixteenth century and no evidence of them in Persian art, until that same time.

However, there is a Bronze Age black pottery jar, crafted sometime between 2200-1600 B.C., that sports clearly recognizable tulips silhouetted in white. Between the time this beautiful vase was crafted and the mid-sixteenth century, the tulip apparently accomplished a Greta Garbo recluse routine that resulted in its virtual disappearance in art and literature for about 3,000 years.

Gerard and Parkinson noticed this gap and thought perhaps Dioscorides's Saturion was really a tulip, but modern scholars now doubt this. There have also been various theories that the Biblical Rose of Sharon was a mountain tulip, but there is too much uncertainty connected to this instance of botanical sleuthing to label it any more than theorizing.

This dearth of information about tulips ends sometime in the mid-sixteenth century when de Busbecq began his famous tenure as ambassador to the court of Suleiman the Great. His contribution to tulip tales is well known and much written about, so perhaps it is interesting to focus upon another person involved in the international events that came to play during tulip's early European days.

Although Clusius did not introduce tulips to Europe, he is credited with making them a horticultural phenomenon. Sometimes referred to as Charles de L'Ecluse (1526–1609), this pioneering botanist was born in Arras, a city in northern France in the area once called Flanders. It was a time of religious persecution: Clusius's parents professed their Protestant faith and

Many tulips and narcissuses can be crammed into a small bed to make a nice springtime show.

promptly had their property confiscated. This just predated the large-scale persecution of other French speaking Protestants who eventually fled to England. They were artisans and merchants, a skilled and resourceful lower middle class, and they brought with them a love of gardening and an obsession with growing perfect flowers.

The loss of the gardens of France was England's gain. Early in the sixteenth century, Henry VIII had gotten his celebrated divorce, declared himself and England independent of the Pope, and promptly split up England's monasteries. When the monks were forced to disband, the art of gardening, which had been the special reserve of religious orders, was largely lost. The French and Flemish refugees rescued England from a bleak gardenless period when they arrived with their horticultural skills. It was they who were responsible for the evolution of the old-time art of floristry, and it was Clusius and early botanists like him who passed on this botanical legacy.

The migration of the Huguenots was not really in full swing until the last quarter of the sixteenth century. In 1551, Clusius was able to escape persecution by moving south from Flanders to settle in Montpellier. There he began a serious study of botany, launching a career that lasted more than a half century.

Clusius collected plants in southern France (1550), Spain and Portugal (1536–64), and Austria and Hungary (c. 1575), but he did not visit Turkey or any Eastern countries where many bulbs grow wild. He wrote that he received his first tulip seeds and bulbs about 1573 while he was in Bruges organizing the work from his collecting trip to Spain. They came to him from Dr. Jean Craton, who had gotten them from de Busbecq, who was Ferdinand I's ambassador to the Turkish court (of Suleiman the Great) from 1554 to 1562.

However, 1573 is not considered the tulip's official introduction. Years earlier, the Swiss botanist Conrad Gesner had illustrated a tulip grown from Turkish seed in *De Hortis Germaniae* (1561). It was this plant, *Tulipa gesnerana,* that Linnaeus christened, and that is the ancestor of most modern tulips.

Between organizing his Spanish plants, receiving his first tulip seeds and bulbs, then moving to Vienna, 1573 was a banner year for Clusius. In Vienna he worked at the court of Maximillan II, who inherited the throne of Ferdinand I and the royal tulip collection, but this job ended in 1576 when Maximillan II died.

That year Clusius gathered up the notes from his Spanish plant expeditions and published a book. He was still passionately studying bulbs in 1601 when his most influential work, *Rariorum Plantarum Historia,* was printed. This work included detailed descriptions of many species of tulips, anemones, cyclamens, and even bulbs from Mexico.

During the period when Clusius was publishing his main body of work, he was also supervising the planting of the Hortus Academicus at Leiden University in Holland. This botanic garden emphasized ornamental rather than pharmaceutical plants and became one of Europe's most influential early research gardens. Clusius soon made a permanent move to Leiden as a professor of botany, and nestled among his household goods he packed his precious tulip bulbs and seeds. His plan was to provide himself with much-needed extra cash by selling off his tulip treasure. And at this point in Clusius's history, a weird story pops up. At least two sources say the Dutch did, indeed, want tulips, but instead of buying them from Clusius, they stole them. Furthermore, these sources contend, the tulips were actually distributed throughout Holland by widespread pilfering instead of by the usual, honorable methods.

But a network of tulip thievery seems highly unlikely, especially since Clusius chose to spend the rest of his life in Holland. Years after the alleged dirty deeds, Clusius assumed the position of head of the Leiden Botanic Garden, and he is generally credited with fathering the commercial bulb industry in the Netherlands. Are these the actions of someone who has been terribly wronged and robbed of the profits of his life's work?

Scholars credit Clusius with changing the composition of northern European gardens, especially with the addition of bulbs and tubers from the Near and Middle East. His name is associated with countless classic bulbs

Tulipa clusiana, *named in honor of tulip-lover Clusius, displays the wiles of the wild tulip.*

The popularity of tulips is undimmed even after centuries of skullduggery, financial scandal, and let-them-eat-tulip-seeds extravagance.

Clusius was responsible for fathering the tulip industry. The Daffodil Mart, Gloucester, Virginia.

—fritillarias, irises, anemones, narcissuses, lilies—but especially with tulips. The route of bulbs from the Middle East to Europe is by no means as straightforward as it seems here, and parallel introductory efforts took place in other parts of Europe. But Clusius is the man who appears time and time again in the history of bulbs; it is in his honor that *Tulipa clusiana, Sternbergia clusiana,* and *Crocus clusii* are named. Also, it is Clusius to whom Holland owes its fame as home of the bulb, for it is there that he did his most important bulb promoting.

And to touch for the barest moment on well-trampled ground, it was there, about twenty-five years after Clusius's death, that the phenomenon of tulipomania raged.

Tulips fared pretty well (without causing economic destruction) in other parts of the world during their debut years. They went from Holland to England in the late 1500s. Plant explorer John Tradescant the Elder (also the Marquis of Salisbury's head gardener) claimed fifty varieties in his Lambeth garden, and the marquis himself had them in his garden at Hatfield. Old records there note that "tulip roots" were purchased by Tradescant in Haarlem.

The eccentric, independent English had no truck with tulipomania, but they did have their own tulip fantasies. At one time during the tulip's early period, the English experimented with eating them. Buckner Hollingsworth records Sir Kenelm Digby's tulip-seed recipe: "Take that seedy end (then very tender) and pick from it the little excresscencies about it, and cut it into short

The almost-black tulip
'Queen of the Night' helps
conjure images of nighttime
tulip picnics on Seraglio
Point during the eighteenth-
century Turkish Tulip Age.
These regal flowers bloom at
Stonecrop in Cold Spring,
New York.

pieces, and boil them and dress them as you would do Pease; and they will taste like Pease, and be very savoury."(Ever the tireless historian, Hollingsworth duly notes that when she repeated Digby's recipe, the results tasted more like asparagus than peas. But the reason tulip seeds likely landed on English tables in the first place was not for taste: the bulbs were considered aphrodisiacs, so who could resist trying the seeds as well?

John Parkinson's *Paradisi* (1629) catches the atmosphere of England's fascination with the tulip, and, in the opening pages, features Adam and Eve amongst cyclamen, anemones, colchicums, and tulips. Such was the impact of this carriage-trade book of pretty and fashionable flowers that, just a few years later, a good tulip collection was an absolute must if you wanted to hold your head up in society—the more formal the tulip the better.

The early tulip became associated with strict upper-class conventionality, but this was not true in other parts of the world. There was also a Tulip Age in Turkey, but there it was more connected to a larger artistic tradition, rather than just social status. Although tulips had been grown by the Ottomans from the start of the sixteenth century, it wasn't until the eighteenth century that a real cult of the tulip took hold. This, no doubt, was a sort of boomerang effect from the earlier European tulipomania, but made such an impact upon decorative arts and literature that it is now known as the Tulip Age.

Ahmed III, Sultan of Turkey from 1703 to 1730, was crazy about tulips—and an extraordinary host. He commissioned special April picnic gardens to be built on Seraglio Point and there he created the ultimate tulip fantasy. His guests would gather for nighttime feasts amid tulip gardens illuminated by candles, oil lamps backed with mirrors, and pet tortoises harnessed with tiny lights who were left to lumber freely like slow-moving will-o'-the-wisps among the flowers. Ahmed

Tulips in the Cooper's garden at Colonial Williamsburg. Although the tulip was an early introduction to colonial American gardens, this country was too young and too poor to participate in a financial floral frenzy of tulipomania.

142

Tulips are also used in more formal bedding schemes at the Governor's Palace at Colonial Williamsburg.

III's successor, Mahmut I, carried on Turkish floral tradition and was known for building garden pyramids upon which were placed lush arrangements of tulips, oil lamps, caged songbirds, and glass balls filled with colored liquids.

All told, during the Tulip Age in Turkey, there were no less than 1,323 tulip varieties available for cultivation. The Turks loved the tulip, but the Europeans craved it, and, for all the hysteria, actually desired it only for a brief period. What had become popular only because of the whims of fashion would eventually become *un*popular because of the whims of fashion, too.

After tulipomania, the popularity of the tulip in Europe went into decline, with its eventual fall from grace so deep that it had to be saved from near-extinction. This was accomplished by none other than the English florists, whose ancestors in trade, if not in blood, were the Flemish and Huguenot refugees from Clusius's homeland. Perhaps because of their own history, the florists had a special sympathy for the now unpopular tulip. They cherished their tulips—breeding, selecting, and growing—and it is through their efforts that the tulip is today a widely available and generally popular garden flower.

Although America was too young to participate in the vicissitudes of the tulip, tulip bulbs were early additions to colonial gardens. Around the time that Ahmed III was throwing his amazing tulip parties, the first Dutch settlers brought bulbs to the New World, and later, Thomas Jefferson grew them at Monticello. Colonial gardeners usually followed the horticultural practices current in that period—namely, digging up all the bulbs after flowering, storing and dividing them, and replanting all in the autumn. This method of planting tulips each autumn has been slow to disappear. Although it does have merits in formal garden schemes, there are other, easier, ways and means with tulips.

Stylewise, among the most recent trends in tulips is a movement back to the more perfumed smaller flowered (and often more delicately colored) species of botanical tulips. There are about 180 species of tulips now recognized, and as each year passes, more of these will appear in bulb catalogues. There is nothing more refreshing than springtime colonies of these unusual little tulips, and as long as one makes absolutely sure the seller has nothing to do with collecting in the wild, they should be planted in quantities as large as financially possible. Three species readily available, inexpensive, and easy to grow are the red-and-white-striped *Tulip clusiana* (named, of course, for tulip hero Clusius), the yellow-and-white *T. tarda,* and the light-purplish-pink *T. saxatilis.* If one is only accustomed to the large, solidly colored tulip hybrids most often on view, these species offer sweet peeks back to the past charms of the tulip.

Miss Jekyll grew wild, or species, tulips in her garden, both "the very desirable" *T. clusiana* and the later-flowering *T. tarda. T. clusiana* is also known as Lady Tulip or Candy Tulip, both names probably arising from this flower's delicate red and white stripes, but *Tulipa clusiana* is easy to remember and say, and gives tribute where it is due. Although at least one source

A modern selection of **Tulipa saxatilis**—*with closed* **T. clusiana** *in center—in Colonial Williamsburg, Virginia.*

Starbursts of the wild **Tulipa tarda** *light up the late-spring garden.*

gives it a very late introduction date of 1802, most agree that this native of Iran, Iraq, and Afganistan was in Europe by the mid-1600s. It is very hardy, blooming in most gardens sometime around April and May, and is a foolproof way to brighten a patch of spring earth.

T. clusiana can be forced and, with its peppermint-stick-like markings, should be a logical addition to the Christmas mantel piece. However, it does seem that in the past, too many instructions for forcing have focused upon Christmas, a time when lots of other festive decorations are readily available. Perhaps it is a good idea to remember the dreary days of March and set a few pots of *T. clusiana* aside to cheer up that distinctly unfestive time of year.

Another pretty and easy species tulip is *T. tarda* (sometimes still listed as *T. dasystemon*). True to its name, it is a late bloomer, and some gardeners consider this a drawback. However, as each small bulb produces up to five sunny yellow flowers, *T. tarda* should not be

Because they usually have shorter stems and smaller flowers, species tulips make excellent choices for forcing. These, purchased as **T. linifolia,** *were probably misidentified, but lovely nonetheless.*

left out of the springtime garden. It may be last but it is definitely not least.

T. tarda is native to Turkestan but appears to be a rather late European introduction (1905?). It is hardy in zones 4 through 8, and has been known to naturalize as far north as Minnesota. This charmer is even stalwart enough for New York City street plantings, so there is bound to be an unpromising area in your garden that could do with a bit of *T. tarda* sunshine.

T. saxatilis is small, and has soft pinkish–purple petals marked at the base with yellow. It is from Crete but does not seem to have been introduced until 1827. (After all the ruckus tulips raised, these late introduction dates are puzzling.) The colors actually may vary from

Those who abhor marshalled lines of perfect tulips should experiment with more cottage-y type plantings such as this one in Emma Morgan's Long Island garden.

deep red to rosy pink, but all varieties are sweetly fragrant. *T. saxatilis* is hardy to zone 4, and has the added convenient characteristic of not needing as much cold weather as other species tulips do.

Species tulips are simply smashing as forced bulbs. Pot up your bulbs in autumn, place pot and all into a plastic bag, and put the whole shebang in an out-of-the-way spot in your refrigerator. They should be kept at about 36 degrees for at least one month. During this time you need do nothing except make sure that no zealous refrigerator-cleaner-outer makes the familiar war cry—"Yuck! What on earth is this?"—as he prepares to throw the whole thing away.

After this cooling period, move the tulip pots to your cold, dark basement (about 40 degrees is ideal), remove the plastic bag, and water. Water each week, and after about another month, leaves will appear and your species tulips can finally join you in the land of the living. Keep them in a cool, light place and watch as their delicate leaves and pretty flowers develop. It's an entirely different show from the bigger, hybrid tulips, but infinitely more charming.

Species tulips are your best bet when trying to accomplish what bulb growers are now calling "tulip perennialization." Someone once glibly defined perennials as "plants which, had they not died, would have come back every year," but it is possible to keep your species tulips going year after year. (This feat is just about hopeless with hybrids, so don't waste your time.) The trick to perennialization is to make the tulips feel as much at home as possible. The worst you can do is put them in the border with other herbaceous-type perennials. Rich soil, abundant summer waterings, and soil-disturbing activities such as weeding and cultivation will toll the death knell for these little guys. Tulips prefer to bake undisturbed in the sun, and actually enjoy near-drought summer conditions.

Many modern gardeners decline to plant tulips because they see no grace or imagination in geometric arrays of brightly colored bloom. But by choosing the species tulips, and allowing them to gradually "plant themselves" where they like, one can attain an artless springtime effect that doubtless was the very root of this flower's fascination.

Even Louise Beeber Wilder, who claimed, "My gardening life began with a prejudice against tulips," later came to love them through an epiphany with some naturalized tulips. She wrote that when passing an abandoned garden she saw "an ancient apple tree that seemed, with everything wreathed in fragrant blossom, to stand lost in an ecstatic dream of its departed youth. Beneath it in the fresh grass, crowding between the crimson peony shoots, were swaying hosts of little scarlet tulips. Thus carelessly disposed beneath the radiant boughs they showed such matchless grace, such piquant vivacity, that I was loathe to go, and lingered full of delight at this choice bit of April's fancy. . . ."

This is definitely the line to take with tulips.

147

Zantedeschia: Araceae

ès

Z. AETHIOPICA—CALLA LILY, TRUMPET LILY

When it comes to grand finales, few flowers have equaled the finesse of the Calla Lily. Although its nickname relegates it to a position near the beginning of an alphabetical listing, this prima donna changed its name not once, but twice, finally settling upon *Zantedeschia aethiopica,* to place itself in a prime position for the curtain's final fall. Of all bulbs, the Calla Lily is the one that looks most able to take a deep, arms-flung-wide curtsy. Listen to a recording of Maria Callas as you gaze at a vase of Callas. It could mark the swan song of humdrum horticulture.

In the past, the Calla Lily was associated with another kind of grand finale—the funeral. No one seems quite sure why, but perhaps because it was so popular during the Victorian period, an era noted for its fascination with death. Or perhaps it made a loftier association through its other name, Trumpet Lily, and was a reminder of the Archangel Gabriel and his trumpet. The most logical reason for the use of Calla Lilies at funerals is that they can be forced to bloom year-round, so were always handy for the unexpected solemn occasion. This morbid link now seems to have gone the way of widow's weeds and mourning jewelry. A perfectly healthy bride can use Callas as wedding decorations and no one will raise an eyebrow.

The Calla Lily looks like a flower designed by Tiffany —like a piece of handmade vellum cut and rolled by an sculptor. These flowers were important Art Deco motifs and also were given center stage in many of Georgia O'Keeffe's paintings. It's a wonder Jesse Helms has never tried to have exhibits of O'Keeffe's Calla paintings suppressed before they could be seen by the young and impressionable. One look at O'Keeffe's Callas and you forget about the funereal end of life and begin to think about the more exciting beginning of it.

Callas get their "come-hither" appearance by way of their membership in the Arum Family. Jack-in-the-pulpits and arum lilies (as well as the usually nonflowering caladiums and colocasias) are also members of this large family. The "flower" is actually a highly modified leaf called a spathe that wraps around a central spike, the spadix, that is covered with small, closely packed flowers.

If it weren't so downright lovely, the Calla Lily might be a prime candidate for an identity crisis: it is not in the Genus *Calla* (*Calla palustris,* a North American native, is the only true *Calla* species), and it is not a lily. *Zantedeschia,* with about six species native to Africa, is the proper name for the genus, this being a final correction after Linnaeus mistakenly placed them in *Calla.* From there they moved further along in the alphabet to the genus *Richardia,* named after French botanist L. C. Richard, but eventually ended up with the far more theatrical sounding *Zantedeschia.* But facing reality (just this once), no matter how well you can rattle off *Zan-*

Zantedeschia aethiopica *is the diva of the bulb world.*

149

🪷

*In South Africa, the aquatic
Calla grows wild in streams
and bogs. Photographed here
at the Alhambra in Spain.*

tedeschia aethiopica, you are probably going to end up calling this plant a Calla Lily anyway. No matter how wrong it is, everyone is going to know what you're talking about.

One common name, however, did meet with real opposition in the person of William Robinson: he simply could not stand calling it Lily-of-the-Nile. The Calla, he ranted more than one hundred years ago, was "emphatically a Cape plant not found within 1,000 miles of the Nile." He was equally adamant about the plant's date of introduction, which he put at much earlier than the 1731 that other sources give. And herein lies a tale.

In 1652 the Dutch East India Company established a garden at Table Bay, the harbor of Cape Town, South Africa. Fruits and vegetables of all kinds were grown in this garden, then loaded onto the company's ships as food for the passengers and crew during the long sea journeys to and from the Far East. For its size, Table Bay, bordered on the north by the Kalahari Desert, is richer in native plants than any other place in the world, and by 1679, the Dutch East India Company garden included both edible and ornamental plants from the surrounding countryside.

The area around Table Bay—its streams, wet meadows, and ditches—literally bursts with huge, magnificent stands of Calla Lily. Often towering six feet tall in the wild, its roots were eaten by wild animals in huge quantities. Porcupines especially loved them, and since these prickly foragers were known as "pigs," the Calla had the unfortunate nickname Pig Lily. No wonder this flower experimented later with several other names before finally settling on one that commands respect.

With all the excitement of porcupines gobbling up flowers growing taller than most people, Callas must have been among the very first native plants to capture the attention of the Dutch East India Company gardeners. And since this plant is a cinch to transport as a tuber, it is entirely conceivable that Callas could have made it to Europe as early as 1687, Robinson's date. (*Nerine sarniensis,* the bulb that plays a mysterious role in the life of *Lycoris,* is another Table Bay bulb transported via Dutch East India Company ships to Europe in the mid-1600s.) Although most other Table Bay introductions didn't hit Europe until after 1700, it's hard to believe that anyone could live in the area and ignore Callas for five minutes, much less almost five decades.

The Calla Lily was enormously popular in Victorian times, a book from the period stating: "This old favorite is so generally known that any description is unnecessary." The root word for the nickname is from *kallos,* "beauty," the same word that gave us *Hemerocallis* for the daylily. And although the Calla Lily appears to have been ubiquitous throughout the 1800s, it seems not to have been taken for granted; in the Victorian language of flowers, it signified "Magnificent Beauty." For once the language of flowers seems to have had some logical basis, although it is rare to see cultivated specimens reach the six-foot mark that wild ones do. Four feet is not uncommon, though, and the cultivar 'Gigantea' may produce "flowers" (spathes) up to ten inches in length.

In the wild the main flush of flowering occurs September through May and then blooms appear intermittently throughout the year. In the Northern Hemisphere they flower in spring and summer, and although it is possible to keep potted plants in bloom year-round, most sources agree that giving them a drying-off and rest period will mean that the plants can replenish themselves for stronger blooming.

Besides the white *Z. aethiopica* there is the bright gold *Z. elliottiana* and the pink *Z. rehmannii* that Elizabeth Lawrence grew. Two cultivars of *Z. aethiopica* introduced at the end of the 1800s are 'Albo-maculata', the Spotted Calla; and a dwarf calla called 'Little Gem' that is especially suited for pots.

Calla Lilies are now at home on diverse shores. They have naturalized in some parts of Cornwall, England, and in the warmest parts of the United States. They are winter-hardy in zone 8, but gardeners with colder winters must keep them in pots that can be moved to frost-free areas.

Now that you have read the program notes on this amazing diva, it's time to enjoy a performance, which may be staged either indoors or out.

A Victorian gardener described Calla Lily as "one of the best parlor plants we have. Its growth is stately; the flower showy, fragrant, and freely produced; and it seems to defy all the injuries which gas and furnace-heat inflict upon other plants." The desire for novelty plants was also strong, and Tovah Martin, a writer who describes herself as "neo-Victorian," recalls that a "Black Calla" came on the market during this period. Appar-

ently a strong *caveat* was in order, though, because there were two plants sold under that name. Louise Beebe Wilder wrote that her Black Calla, *Arum palaestinum*, produced one large, sweetly scented, brownish-red flower on a vigorous stalk. One can imagine it in a dark parlor, gracing an enormous deep-mahogany piano draped with fringed purple silk scarves. But the Black Calla Martin wrote about is an entirely different kettle of fish. *Amorphophallus rivieri* also has a reddish-brown, calla-like spathe, but it possesses, as Wilder said, "a *fiendish* odor." Imagine those Victorians who unwittingly purchased this Black Calla, only to discover that no one wanted to be in the same room with their prize flower.

For indoor use, the creamy elegance of a white Calla Lily can turn an ordinary window into a dramatic setting. One of the earliest Calla challenges was that, in the wilds of Table Bay, this was essentially an aquatic bulb. How much water did it need to grow and how much water could those enterprising Victorians fit into their already overcrowded parlors? Edward Rand gave the following recommendations in 1863: "Plant six or eight roots in half of an oil cask. Paint it green and put on two iron handles." Others recommended planting Callas in large aquariums. The Victorians were undeterred by these requirements and grew Callas in quantities.

Probably the most practical way to grow them indoors today is to have them in a large unglazed terra-cotta pot that is placed in a larger shallow container filled with water. One pretty effect could be achieved

Callas, blossoming here in a courtyard garden in Seville, Spain, are easy to grow indoors and out in unglazed pots set in water.

The dramatic Calla Lily sings a swan song to bulb boredom. Lady Anne Tree's garden.

Opposite: *Irises in the Provence garden of Baroness Lulu de Waldner.*

by setting the pot of Callas into a terra-cotta birdbath that is glazed cobalt blue or deep green inside. (These are easy to find in gardening catalogues and are designed to rest on the ground, not a pedestal.) For a smaller calla variety, try using a fancier pot and setting it inside that silver-plated punch bowl that has only seen the world outside its box once on your wedding day. It all depends whether you want a Georgia O'Keeffe–Santa Fe look or a Fifth Avenue atmosphere. Whatever you do, remember that the Calla is a diva, so use yours to create a scene.

Calla Lilies stir up a lot of drama outdoors, too, and if you are lucky enough to have water in your garden, you can use this bulb to become the Zeffirelli of the garden. And if hiring a backhoe to dredge your pond seems like going overboard, hear what witty, prolific postwar garden writer Beverley Nichols wrote: "If you think that water is of no importance, answer me this question: how is it that whenever the garden is open to the public the crowds automatically drift to the pond, and stay there until sometimes they have to be asked to move away? . . . Why do old ladies sit by the side of it dreaming and young girls stand there as though they were in a trance?"

Add Calla Lilies to the magic of water and you will have a garden scene so compelling that visitors will break into spontaneous applause before allowing themselves to drift away into the romantic atmosphere you have made.

Scores of discerning gardeners before you have been smitten by Callas. William Robinson's *The English Flower Garden* has a beautiful engraving of a large pond with Calla Lilies in Trelissisk, Truro. That lovable bulb lover E. A. Bowles grew them in the deep end of his pond, against a backdrop of dark yew draped in ivy, "the whole group making a charming picture that has painted itself without any aid from my hand save respect for its scheme and a studied neglect." Miss Jekyll was especially fond of the 'Crowborough' Calla Lily, a naturally occuring variety found growing in a garden in Crowborough, England. It is hardy in many parts of the British Isles and was one of Jekyll's favorite cutting flowers.

For real drama you could try pots of Calla Lily plunged into a fountain basin. Or you could orchestrate the following garden signature piece. Create a square or rectangular rock-lined pool with stepped banks. Then position pots of Callas so that they descend the watery stairs like proud Aïdas progressing to the tomb. It would be the grandest of garden gestures, one bound to bring shouts of "Brava! Bravo!" from everyone who experiences it. And it would just go to prove, once again, that there is a marvelous lot of magic to be had from a wrinkled brown root.

SOURCES

Where to Find the Flowers

Compiled with *Andersen Horticultural Library List of Plants and Seeds*

All bulbs included in this book are available from the following mailorder sources. . . .

Acidanthera bicolor
ZONES 8–11
Jung Seed; Park Seed; Multiflora Import; International Bulb

Allium aflatunense
ZONES 4–9
Burpee; White Flower Farm; Andre Viette; McClure & Zimmerman; Smith & Hawken

Allium cepa
ZONES 5–9
(Egyptian Walking)
Nichols Garden Nursery

Cut flowers from winter-forced bulbs.

Allium christophii
ZONES 5–9
McClure & Zimmerman; Park Seed; Thompson & Morgan; Van Engelen; Smith & Hawken

Allium giganteum
ZONES 4–9
McClure & Zimmerman; Wayside Gardens; International Bulb; White Flower Farm; Green Lady; Smith & Hawken

Allium karataviense
ZONES 4–8
McClure & Zimmerman; Maplethorpe; Green Lady

Allium moly
ZONES 4–9
McClure & Zimmerman; Honeywood Lilies; White Flower Farm; Van Engelen; Green Lady

Allium tuberosum
ZONES 4–8
Richters; Heirloom Gardens; High Altitude Gardens; Fragrant Path; Johnny's Selected Seeds; Montrose Nursery

Allium ursinum
ZONES 4–9
Wayside Gardens; Green Lady

Anemone coronaria 'De Caen'
ZONES 7–9
Park Seed; McClure & Zimmerman; International Bulb; Mellingers; Smith & Hawken

Begonia grandis
ZONES 6–9
Hudson Seedsman; Montrose Nursery; Eastern Plant
Specialists; Roslyn Nursery; Kurt Bluemel; Winterthur

Caladium × hortulanum
ZONE 11
Caladium World

Canna indica
ZONES 8–11
Thompson & Morgan

Iris-breeding fields in Somerset, England.

Chasmanthe aethiopica
ZONES 8–10
Bioquest International; Green Lady

Colchicum autumnale
ZONES 5–9
Hudson Seedsman; Charles Mueller; Richters; Thompson &
Morgan

Colchicum speciosum
ZONES 5–9
McClure & Zimmerman; Smith & Hawken

Colocasia esculenta
ZONES 9–11
Park Seed; Lilypons Water Gardens; William Tricker;
Aldridge Nursery

Crocus chrysanthus
ZONES 4–8
Green Lady; Smith & Hawken

Crocus speciosus
ZONES 5–9
McClure & Zimmerman; Burpee; Wayside Gardens; White
Flower Farm

Crocus vernus
ZONES 4–8
Green Lady; Smith & Hawken

Cyclamen coum
ZONES 7–9
Siskiyou Rare Plant Nursery; Wayside Gardens; Montrose
Nursery; Russell Graham

Cyclamen hederifolium
ZONES 5–9
Nichols Garden Nursery; Bluebird Nursery; Wayside
Gardens; Montrose Nursery; Roslyn Nursery; Rice Creek
Gardens; Rocknoll Nursery

Cyclamen persicum
ZONES 9–10
Thompson & Morgan; Montrose Nursery

Cyclamen purpurascens
ZONES 5–9
Thompson & Morgan; Montrose Nursery

Fritillaria persica
ZONES 4–9
McClure & Zimmerman; Van Engelen; International Bulb

Hemerocallis citrina
ZONES 3–10
Andre Viette; Corn Hill Nursery

Hemerocallis fulva
ZONES 3–10
Bear Creek Nursery; We-Du Nurseries; Farmer Seed &
Nursery; Messelaar Bulb

Hemerocallis lilioasphodelus
ZONES 4–10
Oregon Bulb Farms; Busse Gardens; Carroll Gardens;
We-Du Nurseries

Hemerocallis minor
ZONES 4–10
We-Du Nurseries; Bluebird Nursery; Midwest
Groundcovers

Hyacinthus orientalis var. *albulus*
ZONES 7–10
Green Lady

Iris danfordiae
ZONES 4–9
McClure & Zimmerman; Van Schaik; Burpee; Peter
DeJager Bulb

Iris ensata
ZONES 5–9
Camellia Forest Nursery; Smith & Hawken

Iris foetidissima
ZONES 6–10
Busse Gardens; Thompson & Morgan; André Viette;
Bluebird Nursery

Iris pallida
ZONES 4–10
André Viette

Iris pseudacorus
ZONES 4–9
Grandview Nursery; Maplethorpe; Cooper's Garden; Sunny
Border Nurseries; Country Wetlands Nursery;
Kurt Bluemel

Iris reticulata
ZONES 4–9
Wayside Gardens; Messelaar Bulb; McClure & Zimmerman;
International Bulb

Iris sibirica
ZONES 3–9
Hudson Seedsman; Borbeleta Gardens; Roslyn Nursery;
Lilypons; Smith & Hawken

Iris xiphioides
ZONES 6–9
Burpee; Park Seed; Wayside Gardens; Smith & Hawken

Lilium auratum
ZONES 5–8
Jung Seed; Thompson & Morgan; Wayside Gardens; Salter
Tree Farm; Multiflora Import

Lilium canadense
ZONES 3–8
Rex Bulb Farms; B & D Lilies

Lilium candidum
ZONES 4–9
Maplethorpe; McClure & Zimmerman; Wayside Gardens;
Messelaar Bulb; International Bulb

Lilium lancifolium
ZONES 5–8
Wayside Gardens; Salter Tree Farm

Lilium regale
ZONES 5–8
B & D Lilies; Wayside Gardens; Fragrant Path; Multiflora
Import; Thompson & Morgan; Plantage

Gladiolus in a New York cutting garden.

Lilium superbum
ZONES 4–8
Salter Tree Farm; Wayside Gardens; Mellingers; Russell Graham

Lycoris radiata
ZONES 7–10
Salter Tree Farm; McClure & Zimmerman; Daffodil Mart; White Flower Farm; Sisters Bulb Farm

Melasphaerula ramosa
ZONES 10–11
Green Lady

Muscari armeniacum
ZONES 3–8
Weller-GM Nurseries; Park Seed; Van Schaik; Van Engelen; Smith & Hawken

Narcissus bulbocodium var. *conspicuus*
ZONES 7–9
McClure & Zimmerman; Burpee; Daffodil Mart; Peter DeJager Bulb; Van Schaik

Narcissus 'King Alfred'
ZONES 3–8
B & D Lilies; Wayside Gardens; McClure & Zimmerman; Messelaar Bulb; Smith & Hawken

Narcissus tazetta var. *orientalis*
ZONES 9–10
Daffodil Mart

Oxalis versicolor
ZONES 8–10
Green Lady

Puschkinia scilloides
ZONES 4–8
McClure & Zimmerman; Park Seed; Burpee; Peter DeJager Bulb

Scilla sibirica
ZONES 3–9
Harris Seeds; Van Schaik; McClure & Zimmerman; Weller-GM Nurseries

Tools of the trade at the Daffodil Mart, Gloucester, Virginia.

Sternbergia clusiana
ZONES 7–9
John D. Lyon; Green Lady

Sternbergia lutea
ZONES 6–9
Charles Mueller; McClure & Zimmerman; Green Lady

Tulipa clusiana
ZONES 4–10
McClure & Zimmerman; Van Schaik; Burpee; Peter DeJager Bulb; Smith & Hawken

Tulipa saxatilis
ZONES 4–9
McClure & Zimmerman; Van Schaik; International Bulb; Smith & Hawken; Peter DeJager Bulb

Tulipa tarda
ZONES 4–8
Honeywood Lilies; McClure & Zimmerman; Burpee; White Flower Farm; Smith & Hawken

Zantedeschia aethiopica
ZONES 9–10
Louisiana Nursery; Park Seed; White Flower Farm; McClure & Zimmerman; Carter Seeds

Nurseries

Aldridge Nursery Inc. (wholesale)
Von Ormy, TX 78073
(512) 622-3491

B & D Lilies
330 P Street
Port Townsend, WA 98368
(206) 385-1738

Bear Creek Nursery
PO Box 4411
Bear Creek Road
Northport, WA 99157

Bioquest International
PO Box 5752
Santa Barbara, CA 93150-5752
(805) 969-4072

Bluebird Nursery Inc. (wholesale)
PO Box 460
521 Linden Street
Clarkson, NE 68629
(402) 892-3457

Kurt Bluemel, Inc.
2740 Greene Lane
Baldwin, MD 21013
(301) 557-7229

Bluebells in the public garden at Wing Haven, Charlotte, North Carolina.

The medieval gardens at the Cloisters Museum in New York City are open to the public.

Borbeleta Gardens Inc.
15980 Canby Avenue
Faribault, MN 55021
(507) 334-2807

W. Atlee Burpee & Co
300 Park Avenue
Warminster, PA 18974
(215) 674-4915

Busse Gardens
Route 2, Box 238
635 East 7th Street
Cokato, MN 55321
(612) 286-2654

Caladium World
PO Drawer 629
Sebring, FL 33817
(813) 385-7661

Camellia Forest Nursery
125 Carolina Forest Road
Chapel Hill, NC 27516
(919) 967-5529

Carroll Gardens
444 East Main Street
PO Box 310
Westminster, MD 21157
(301) 848-5422

Carter Seeds (wholesale)
475 Mar Vista Drive
Vista, CA 92083
(800) 872-7711

Coopers Garden
212 W. County Road C
Roseville, MN 55113
(612) 484-7878

Corn Hill Nursery Ltd
R.R. 5
Petitcodiac, New Brunswick EOA
  2HO
Canada
(506) 756-3635

Country Wetlands Nursery Ltd
Box 126
Muskego, WI 53150
(414) 679-1268

Daffodil Mart
Route 3, Box 794
Gloucester, VA 23061
(804) 693-3966

Peter DeJager Bulb Co.
PO Box 2010
188 Asburg Street
South Hamilton, MA 01982
(508) 468-4707

Eastern Plant Specialists
Box 226
Georgetown Island, ME 04548
(207) 371-2888

Farmer Seed & Nursery
818 NW 4th Street
Faribault, MN 55021
(507) 334-4162

Fragrant Path
PO Box 328
Fort Calhoun, NE 68023

Russell Graham
4030 Eagle Crest Rd., N.W.
Salem, OR 97304
(503) 362-1135

Grandview Nursery (wholesale)
Route 4, Box 44
Youngsville, LA 70592
(318) 856-5293

Green Lady Gardens
1415 Eucalyptus Drive
San Francisco, CA 94132
(415) 753-3332

Harris Seeds
961 Lyell Avenue
Rochester, NY 14606
(716) 458-2882

Heirloom Gardens
PO Box 138
Guerneville, CA 95446
(707) 869-0967

High Altitude Gardens
PO Box 4238
Ketchum, ID 83340
(208) 726-3221

Honeywood Lilies
PO Box 63
Parkside, Saskatchewan
SOJ 2AO
Canada
(306) 747-3296

J. L. Hudson, Seedsman
PO Box 1058
Redwood City, CA 95064

International Bulb Company Inc.
  (wholesale)
PO Box 545
5 Wortendyke Avenue
Montvale, NJ 07645
(201) 573-0363

Johnny's Selected Seeds
Foss Hill Road
Albion, ME 04910
(207) 437-9294

J. W. Jung Seed Co.
Randolph, WI 53957
(414) 326-3121

Lilypons Water Gardens
6800 Lilypons Road
Lilypons, MD 21717
(301) 874-5133

Louisiana Nursery
Route 7, Box 43
Opelousas, LA 70570
(318) 948-3696

John D. Lyon, Inc.
143 Alewife Brook Parkway
Cambridge, MA 02140
(617) 876-3705

McClure & Zimmerman
108 W. Winnebago
PO Box 368
Friesland, WI 53935
(414) 326-4220

Maplethorpe
11296 Sunnyview NE
Salem, OR 97301
(503) 362-5121

Mellinger's Inc.
2310 W. South Range Road
North Lima, OH 44452
(216) 549-9861

Messelaar Bulb Co. Inc.
PO Box 269, Country Road,
  Route 1-A
Ipswich, MA 01938
(508) 356-3737

*Shiny black seeds give
Blackberry Lily
(Belamcanda chinensis) its
name. Grown here in the
re-created gardens of the
Moravian congregation town
of Old Salem, in Winston-
Salem, North Carolina.*

Midwest Groundcovers (wholesale)
PO Box 748
St. Charles, IL 60174
(312) 742-1790

Montrose Nursery
PO Box 957
Hillsborough, NC 27278
(919) 732-7787

Charles H. Mueller
River Road
Star Route, Box 21
New Hope, PA 18938
(215) 862-2033

Multiflora Import Co. (wholesale)
PO Box 603
Wayzata, MN 55391
(612) 475-1124

Nichols Garden Nursery
1190 No. Pacific Highway
Albany, OR 97321
(503) 928-9280

Oregon Bulb Farms
14071 NE Arndt Road
Dept. MO
Aurora, OR 97002
(503) 678-1272

George W. Park Seed Co., Inc.
Cokesbury Road
Greenwood, SC 29647
(803) 223-7333

Plantage, Inc. (wholesale)
PO Box 28
Cutchogue, NY 11935
(516) 734-6832

Rex Bulb Farms
Box 774
Port Townsend, WA 98368
(206) 385-4280

Rice Creek Gardens
1315 66th Avenue, NE
Minneapolis, MN 55432
(612) 574-1197

Richters
Goodwood, Ontario
LOC 1AO
Canada
(416) 640-6677

Rocknoll Nursery
9210 U.S. 50
Hillsboro, Oh 45133
(513) 393-1278

Roslyn Nursery
211 Burrs Lane
Dix Hills, NY 11746
(516) 643-9347

Salter Tree Farm
Route 2, Box 1332
Madison, FL 32340
(904) 973-6312

Siskiyou Rare Plant Nursery
2825 Cummings Road
Medford, OR 97501
(503) 772-6846

Sisters Bulb Farm
Route 2, Box 170
Gibsland, LA 71028

Smith & Hawken
25 Corte Madera
Mill Valley, CA 94941
(415) 383-2000

*Many bulbs were important in early medicine. Saffron (**Crocus sativus**) is included among these medicinal herbs at **Old Salem, Winston-Salem, North Carolina.***

Sunny Border Nurseries Inc.
  (wholesale)
1709 Kensington Road
PO Box 86
Kensington, CT 06037
(203) 828-0321

Sunnybrook Farms
9448 Mayfield Road
PO Box 6
Chesterland, OH 44026
(216) 729-7232

Thompson & Morgan
PO Box 1308
Jackson, NJ 08527
(201) 363-2225

William Tricker, Inc.
7125 Tanglewood Drive
PO Box 31267
Independence, Oh 44131
(216) 524-3491

Van Engelen Inc. (wholesale)
313 Maple Street
Litchfiled, CT 06759
(203) 567-8734

Mary Mattison Van Schaik
RFD Box 181
Cavendish, VT 05142
(802) 226-7338

Growing fields at the Daffodil
Mart, Gloucester, Virginia.

André Viette Farm and Nursery
Route 1, Box 16
Fishersville, VA 22939
(703) 943-2315

Wayside Gardens
Hodges, SC 29695
(800) 845-1124

We-Du Nurseries
Route 5, Box 724
Marion, NC 28752
(704) 738-8300

Weller-GM Nurseries, Inc.
  (wholesale)
13 W. 16th Street
Holland, MI 49423
(616) 335-5853

White Flower Farm
Litchfield, CT 06759
(203) 496-1661

Winterthur Museum and Gardens
Winterthur, DE 19735
(800) 767-0500

*Dry flowers such as Calla
(Zantedeschia aethiopica)
and Chinese Sacred Lily
(Narcissus tazetta var.
orientalis) by pinning upside
down to a notice board. Grace
Tabor's bulb book was
published in 1912.*

BIBLIOGRAPHY

Addison, Josephine. 1985. *The Illustrated Plant Lore*. London: Sidwick & Jackson.

Andersen Horticulture Library's Source List of Plants and Seeds. 1989. By Richard T. Isaacson and Andersen Horticultural Library. University of Minnesota Libraries.

Anderson, A. W. 1950. *The Coming of the Flowers*. London: Williams & Norgate Ltd.

Bailey, L. H. 1949. *Bailey's Manual of Cultivated Plants*.

Barr, Peter. 1884. *Ye Narcissus or Daffodyl Flowere*. London: Simmons & Botten. Reprint 1968, Washington D.C.: American Daffodil Society.

Bayard, Tania. 1985. *Sweet Herbs and Sundry Flowers: Medieval Gardens and the Gardens of the Cloister*. Boston: David R. Godine.

Beauty from Bulbs. 1930. New York: John Scheepers, Inc.

Bennett, Ida D. 1903. *The Flower Garden: A Handbook of Practical Garden Lore*. New York: McClure, Phillips & Co.

Berkeley, Edmund, and Dorothy Smith Berkeley. 1982. *The Life and Travels of John Bartram: From Lake Ontario to the River St. John*. Tallahassee: University Presses of Florida.

Betts, Edwin M., and Hazlehurst Bolton Perkins. 1986. *Thomas Jefferson's Flower Garden at Monticello*. Revised by Peter J. Hatch. Charlottesville: University of Virginia Press.

Bianchini, Francesco, and Francesco Corbetta. 1975. *The Complete Book of Health Plants: An Atlas of Medicinal Plants*. New York: Crescent Books.

Blanchan, Neltje. 1913. *The American Flower Garden*. New York: Doubleday, Page & Co.

Bourne, Eleanor. 1980. *Heritage of Flowers*. New York: G. P. Putnam's Sons.

Bowles, E. A. 1920. *My Garden in Autumn and Winter*. New York: Dodge Publishing.

———. 1914. *My Garden in Spring*. Reprinted 1971, Vermont: Theophrastus.

———. 1914. *My Garden in Summer*. New York. Dodge Publishing Co.

———. 1924. *A Handbook of Crocus and Colchicum for Gardeners*. London: John Lane. Reprinted 1955, London: Lowe & Brydone.

Breck, Joseph. 1856. *The Flower Garden*. Boston: John P. Jewett.

Brett, Walter. [c. 1900] *News Chronicle: Home Gardening*. London: George Newnes.

Brickell, Christopher, and Fay Sharman. 1986. *The Vanishing Garden: A Conservation Guide to Garden Plants*. London: John Murray and the Royal Horticultural Society.

Bridgeman, Thomas. 1866. *The American Gardener's Assistant*. Philadelphia: Porter & Coates.

Bryan, John E. 1989. *Bulbs. Vols. 1 & 2*. Portland, Ore.: Timber Press.

Bynum, Flora Ann. "The Plant Reporter: Searching for Pink Roman Hyacinths." *Magnolia Bulletin of the Southern Garden History Society,* Summer 1990, Vol. VII, p. 9.

Callaway, Nicholas. 1988. *Georgia O'Keeffe's One Hundred Flowers*. New York: Alfred A. Knopf.

Camps, Wendell, *et al*. 1957. *The World in Your Garden*. Washington, D.C.: National Geographic Society.

Charlesworth, Geoffrey B. 1988. *The Opinionated Gardener*. Boston: David R. Godine.

Clay, Horace F., and James Hubbard. 1987. *Tropical Exotics*. Honolulu: University of Hawaii Press.

Coats, Alice M. 1956. *Flowers and Their Histories*. London: Adam & Charles Black.

Dried Tulipa clusiana, *Rand's* Bulbs *from 1873, and Louise Beebe Wilder's* Adventures *(1936).*

Cook, E. T., ed. [c. 1920] *The Century Book of Gardening: A Comprehensive Work for Every Lover of the Garden.* London: Country Life/George Newness Ltd.

Crowell, Robert L. 1982. *The Lore and Legends of Flowers.* New York: Thomas Y. Crowell.

Culpeper, Nicholas. 1653. *Culpeper's Complete Herbal.* Reprint 1960, Hackensack, N.J.: Wehman.

Davis, Rosalie H. "Forcing Hardy Bulbs." *Horticulture,* Oct. 1989, p. 16.

de Bray, Lys. *Manual of Old Fashioned Flowers.* Somerset, England: Oxford Illustrated Press.

De Hertogh, Dr. A. A., and M. A. Powell. 1990. *Guidelines for Utilization of Summer and Fall Flowering: Bulbs in the U.S. and Canada.* Netherlands: Netherlands Flower Bulb Institute.

De Wolf, Gordon D, *et al.* 1986. *Taylor's Guide to Bulbs.* Boston: Houghton Mifflin.

Duke University Medical Center Library. 1978. *The Medical Garden.* Durham, N.C.:

Earl, Alice Morse. 1901. *Old Time Gardens: A Book of the Sweet of the Year,* New York: Macmillan.

Ely, Helena Rutherford. 1913. *A Woman's Hardy Garden.* New York: Macmillan.

Fairchild, David. 1941. *The World Was My Garden: Travels of a Plant Explorer.* New York: Charles Scribner's Sons.

Farrington, Edward I. 1931. *Ernest H. Wilson: Plant Hunter.* Boston: Stratford Co.

Fish, Margery. 1961. *Cottage Garden Flowers.* London: W. H. & L. Collingridge Ltd. Reprinted 1980, London: David & Charles.

———. 1965. *A Flower for Every Day.* London: Studio Vista. Reprinted 1981, London: David & Charles.

———. 1964. *Ground Cover Plants.* London: W. H. & L. Collingridge Ltd.

———. 1956. *We Made a Garden.* London and Boston: Faber & Faber.

The Floral World. Garden Guide and Country Companion. 1879. London: Groombridge & Sons.

Foy, Jessica. n.d. *Back to Nature: Medicinal Herbs on Dr. Vierling's Inventory.* Old Salem, N.C.: n.p.

Fraser, J., and L. Hemsley. 1846 & 1917. *Johnson's Gardener's Dictionary.* London: George Routledge & Sons.

Garden Guide to the Lower South. 1986. Savannah, Ga.: Trustee Garden Club.

Genders, Roy. 1973. *Bulbs: A Complete Handbook.* London: Robert Hale & Co.

———.1960. *Bulbs All the Year Round.* London: Garden Book Club.

———. (1969) 1984. *The Cottage Garden and the Old-Fashioned Flowers.* London: Pelham Books.

Glattstein, Judy. "Species Tulips." *Flower & Garden,* Sept. 1989, p. 26.

Graf, Alfred Byrd. 1974. *Exotic Plant Manual,* 4th Ed. East Rutherford, N.J.: Roehrs Company.

———— Exotica: *Series Four International.* Vols. 1 & 2. East Rutherford, N.J.: Roehrs Company

Hadfield, Miles, *et al.* 1980. *British Gardeners: A Biographical Dictionary.* London: A. Zwemmer Ltd.

Hagan, Patti. "Truth in Gardening: Uprooting Black-Market Bulbs." *Wall Street Journal,* Jan. 3, 1991.

Haldane, Elizabeth A. 1934. *Scots Gardens in Old Times (1200–1800).* London: Alexander MacLehose & Co.

Halleux, Carmelia. "The Medieval Garden and Its Role in Medicine." In *Medieval Gardens,* ed. Elizabeth Mac-Dougall. Washington, D.C.: Dumbarton Oaks Research Library and Collection.

Hampden, Mary. 1921. *Bulb Gardening.* London: Thorton Butterworth Ltd.

Hay, Roy. 1985. *The Readers Digest Encyclopaedia of Garden Plants and Flowers.* London: Readers Digest Association.

Henderson, Peter. 1904. *Henderson's Bulb Culture.*

————. 1890. *Henderson's Handbook of Plants and General Horticulture.* New York: Peter Henderson & Co.

Herwig, Rob. 1975. *One Hundred and Twenty-eight Bulbs You Can Grow.* New York: Collier Macmillan.

Heywood, V. H. 1978. *Flowering Plants of the World.* Englewood Cliffs, N.J.: Prentice-Hall.

Hibberd, Shirley. 1871. *The Amateur's Flower Garden.* London: Groombridge & Sons. Reprinted 1986, Kent, England: Croom Helm Ltd.

————. 1874. *The Floral World and Garden Guide.* London: Groombridge & Sons.

Hobhouse, Penelope. 1985. *Gertrude Jekyll on Gardening.* New York: Vintage Books.

Hollingsworth, Buckner. 1958. *Flower Chronicles.* New Brunswick, N.J.: Rutgers University Press.

————. 1962. *Her Garden Was Her Delight.* New York: Macmillan.

Horton, Alvin, and James McNair. 1986. *All About Bulbs.* San Francisco: Chevron Chemical Co.

Hortus Third. 1976. By the Staff of the Liberty Hyde Bailey Hortorium. New York: Macmillan.

Jekyll, Gertrude. 1907. *Flower Decoration in the House.* London: Country Life Ltd.

————. 1901. *Lilies for English Gardens: A Guide for Amateurs.* Reprinted 1982, Suffolk England: Antique Collector's Club.

Jellicoe, Sir Geoffrey, and Susan Jellicoe. 1986. *The Oxford Companion to Gardens.* New York: Oxford University Press.

Johnson, Hugh. 1979. *The Principles of Gardening.* New York: Simon & Schuster.

Kirby, A. M. 1914. *Daffodils & Narcissus and How to Grow Them.* New York: Doubleday, Page & Co.

Lacy, Allen. 1990. *The Garden in Autumn.* New York: Atlantic Monthly Press.

————. 1984. *Home Ground: A Gardener's Miscellany.* New York: Ballantine Books.

————. "On Bearding the Iris: Color It Anything." *New York Times,* June 7, 1990, Home Section, C1.

Lancaster, Roy. 1989. *Travels in China: A Plantsman's Paradise.* Suffolk, England: Antique Collector's Club.

Lawrence, Elizabeth. 1961. *Gardens in Winter*. New York: Harper & Brothers.

————. 1987. *Gardening for Love: The Market Bulletins*. Durham: Duke University Press.

————. 1957. *The Little Bulbs: A Tale of Two Cities*. New York: Criterion Books.

————. 1971. *Lob's Wood*. Ohio: Board of Trustees of Cincinnati Nature Centre.

————. 1942. *A Southern Garden: A Handbook for the Middle South*. Chapel Hill: University of North Carolina Press. Reprinted 1984.

Leighton, Ann. 1986. *American Gardens in the Eighteenth Century: For Use or for Delight*. Amherst: University of Massachusetts Press.

————. 1987. *American Gardens in the Nineteenth Century: For Comfort and Affluence*. Amherst: University of Massachusetts Press.

————. 1986. *Early American Gardens: for Meate or Medicine*. Amherst: University of Massachusetts Press.

Little, G. Allan. 1981. *Scotland's Gardens*. Spur Books: Scotland's Garden Scheme.

Long, Elias A. 1896. *Ornamental Gardening for Americans*. New York: Orange Judd Co.

Lovejoy, Ann. "Tulips That Triumph." *Horticulture Magazine,* Oct. 1988, p. 34.

McCurdy, Robert M. 1917. *Garden Flowers*. New York: Doubleday, Doran.

McDonough, Mark. "Alliums in the Garden." *Pacific Horticulture,* Winter 1986, pp. 46–51.

MacFadyen, J. Trevor. "Strains of Brilliance." *Horticultrue,* April 1987, p. 31.

McFarland, J. Horace, *et al.* 1945. *Garden Bulbs in Color*. New York: Macmillan.

McHoy, Peter. 1988. *Gardener's Encyclopedia of Bulbs*. New York: Gallery Books (W.H. Smith).

McIlvaine, Frances Edge. 1928. *Spring in the Little Garden*. Boston: Little, Brown & Co.

McKinney, Ella Porter. 1927. *Iris in the Little Gardens*. Boston: Little, Brown & Co.

MacSelf, A. J. 1935. *Saunders Flower Garden*. London: Collingridge.

Mallary, Peter, and Frances Mallary. 1986. *A Redouté Treasury: 468 Watercolors from Les Liliacées*. New York: Vendome Press.

Martin, Tovah. 1988. *Once upon a Windowsill: A History of Indoor Plants*. Oregon: Timber Press.

Massingham, Betty. 1982. *A Century of Gardeners*. London: Faber & Faber.

Mitchell, Henry. "For the Love of Iris." *Horticulture,* Dec. 1987, p. 20.

Mitchell's Bulb Growing Guide. [c. 1910.] Philadelphia, PA: Henry F. Mitchell Co.

Nichols, Beverley. 1932. *Down the Garden Path*. London: Jonathan Cape.

————. 1963. *Garden Open Today*. New York: E. P. Dutton & Co.

————. 1951. *Merry Hall*. London: Jonathan Cape.

Nicholson, George. 1885. *The Illustrated Dictionary of Gardening*. London: L. Upcott Gill.

Nicholson, Philippa. 1983. *Vita Sackville-West's Garden Book*. New York: Atheneum.

Page, Russell. 1962. *The Education of a Gardener*. Reprinted 1983, New York: Random House.

Parke, Margaret. "Pride of Place." *Horticulture,* Nov. 1987, p. 32.

Dried white Roman Hyacinths (Hyacinthus orientalis *var.* albulus) *and books from the author's collection.*

Paterson, Allen. 1985. *Herbs in the Garden*. Reprinted 1990, London: Dent & Sons Ltd.

Perry, Frances. 1972. *Flowers of the World*. New York: Hamlyn.

Pickles, Sheila. 1989. *The Language of Flowers*. New York: Harmony Books.

Powell, Claire. 1979. *The Meaning of Flowers: Plant Lore and Symbolism from Popular Custom and Literature*. Boulder, Colo.: Shambhala.

Quinn, Carey E. 1959. *Daffodils, Outdoors and In*. New York: Hearthside Press.

Ramsdall, Mary. "Adding A Point to It: Irises." *The Hardy Plant,* Vol. 10, No. 1 (Spring 1988), p. 10.

Rand, Edward Sprague. 1873. *A Treatise on Hardy and Tender Bulbs and Tubers*. Boston: Shepard & Gill.

Randall, Colvin. 1987. *Longwood Gardens*. York, Pa.: York Graphic Services.

Rix, Martyn, and Roger Phillips. 1981. *The Bulb Book*. London: Pan Books.

———. 1983. *Growing Bulbs*. London: Christopher Helm. Portland, Ore.: Timber Press.

Robinson, William. 1883. *The English Flower Garden and Home Grounds*. London: John Murray.

———. 1870. *The Wild Garden: Naturalization and Natural Grouping of Hardy Exotic Plants*. Reprinted 1983, London: Century Publishing.

Rohde, Elanor Sinclair. 1922. *The Old English Herbals*. London: Longmans, Green. Reprinted 1971, New York: Dover Publications.

Rossi, Rossela. 1989. *Guide to Bulbs*. New York: Simon & Schuster.

Seymour, E.L.D. 1949. *Favorite Flowers in Color*. New York: H. Wise & Co.

Shelton, Louise. 1915. *Beautiful Gardens in America*. New York: Charles Scribner's Sons.

Silberrad, Una, and Sophie Lyall. 1909. *Dutch Bulbs and Gardens*. London: Adam and Charles Black.

Sitwell, Sacheverell. 1939. *Old Fashioned Flowers*. London: Country Life Ltd.

———, and Wilfrid Blunt. 1990. *Great Flower Books 1700–1900*. New York: Atlantic Monthly Press.

Slossen, Elvenia. 1951. *Pioneer American Gardening*. New York: Coward-McCann.

Stuart, David, and James Sutherland. 1987. *Plants from the Past*. New York: Viking. Middlesex, England: Penguin Books.

Stufano, Marco Polo. "Wave Hill," in Rosemary Verey, 1990, *The American Man's Garden*. Boston: Little, Brown & Co.

Tabor, Grace. 1912. *Making a Bulb Garden*. New York: McBride, Nast & Co.

———. 1913. *Old Fashioned Gardening: A History and a Reconstruction*. New York: McBride, Nast & Co.

Tay Eng Pin *et al*. 1989. *Pictorial Guide to Singapore Botanic Gardens*. Singapore Botanic Gardens.

Taylor, Raymond L. 1952. *Plants of Colonial Days*. Williamsburg: Colonial Williamsburg Press.

Thacker, Christopher. 1979. *The History of Gardens*. Los Angeles: University of California Press.

Thaxter, Celia. 1894. *An Island Garden*. Reprinted 1984, Ithaca: Bullbrier Press.

Thomas, Graham Stuart. 1976. *Perennial Garden Plants or The Modern Florilegium*. London: J. M. Dent & Sons.

Thomas, H. H. 1912. *The Complete Gardener*. London: Cassell & Co.

Tice, Patricia M. 1984. *Gardening in America 1830–1910*. Rochester, N.Y.: Strong Museum.

Van Ravenswaay, Charles. 1977. *A Nineteenth Century Garden*. New York: Universe Books.

Waters, George. "The Winter Iris." *Pacific Horticulture,* Spring 1989, p. 1.

Watson, Forbes. 1901. *Flowers and Gardens: Notes on Plant Beauty*. London: John Lane, The Bodley Head.

Weinreb, Herman. "New Use for a Time Tested Botanical". *Garden,* November–December 1986, p. 16.

Weston, T. A. 1926. *Bulbs That Bloom in the Spring*. New York: A. T. De La Mare Co.

Wilder, Louise Beebe. 1936. *Adventures with Hardy Bulbs*. New York: Macmillan.

———. 1932. *The Fragrant Garden*. New York: Macmillan. Reprinted, New York: Dover, 1974.

———. 1925. *Adventures in My Garden and Rock Garden*. New York: Doubleday, Page & Co.

———. 1918. *Color in My Garden*. Reprinted 1990, New York: Atlantic Monthly Press.

Williams, Henry T. 1873. *Window Gardening: The Culture of Flowers and Ornamental Plants*. New York: Henry T. Williams.

Wister, John C. 1930. *Bulbs for American Gardens*. Boston: Stratford Co.

Wright, Richardson. 1924. *The Practical Book of Outdoor Flowers*. New York: Garden City Publishing Co.

———. 1934. *The Story of Gardening from the Hanging Gardens of Babylon to the Hanging Gardens of New York*. New York: Dodd, Mead & Co.

———. 1934. *The Winter Diversions of a Gardener*. Philadelphia: J. B. Lippincott Co.

Yang, Linda. 1990. *The City Gardener's Handbook: From Balcony to Backyard*. New York: Random House.

Yepsen, R. B., Jr. 1984. *The Encyclopedia of Natural Insect and Disease Control*. Pennsylvania: Rodale Press.

USDA PLANT HARDINESS ZONE MAP

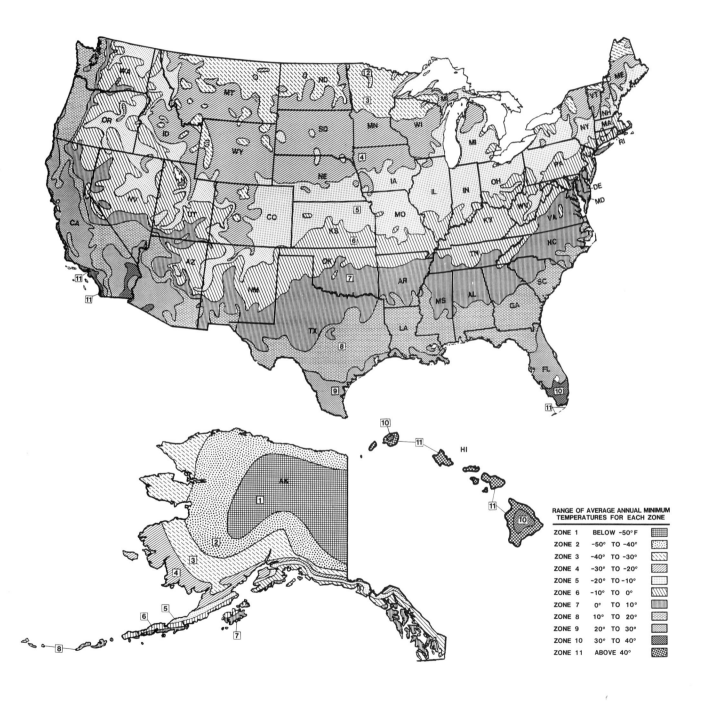

RANGE OF AVERAGE ANNUAL MINIMUM TEMPERATURES FOR EACH ZONE	
ZONE 1	BELOW -50° F
ZONE 2	-50° TO -40°
ZONE 3	-40° TO -30°
ZONE 4	-30° TO -20°
ZONE 5	-20° TO -10°
ZONE 6	-10° TO 0°
ZONE 7	0° TO 10°
ZONE 8	10° TO 20°
ZONE 9	20° TO 30°
ZONE 10	30° TO 40°
ZONE 11	ABOVE 40°

173

INDEX

Numerals in *italics* indicate illustrations.

A

acidanthera, xxi, 2–5, *2–5*
Acidanthera bicolor, 2, *2,* 3, 157
agapanthus, 29
Algerian Iris, 84
Alhambra, Spain, *150*
allium, *ix,* xxiii, 6–12, *6–13*
   Chinese Chive, 7, 12, *13*
   Egyptian Onion, *8,* 9
   Lily Leek, 11–12
   Ramsons, 12, *12–13*
   Stars of Persia, *9,* 11
Allium, 6–12, *6–13*
   aflatunense, 10, 11, 157
   ascalonicum, 6
   cepa (Proliferum Group), 6, *8,* 9, 157
   christophii, 9, 11, 157
   fistulosum, 6
   giganteum, 9, 11, 157
   karataviense, 11, *11,* 157
   magicum, 9
   moly, 11–12, 157
   neopolitanum, 11
   nigrum, 9
   porrum, 6
   sativum, 6
   schoenoprasum, 6
   tuberosum, 7, 12, *13,* 157
   ursinum, 12, *12–13,* 157

Amaryllidaceae, 6–12, *6–13,* 98–101, *99–101,* 108–19, *109–19,* 130–35, *131–35*
amaryllis, 130
'Ambassadeur' bearded iris, 69
American Bloodroot, *vi*
Amorphophallus rivieri, 152
anemone, *xxii,* 14–19, *14–19,* 41
   Florist's, 14
Anemone, 14–19, *14–19*
   apennina, 18
   blanda, 18
   coronaria, 14–19, *14–19,* 144, 157
Angel-wings, 28
Araceae, 26–29, *26–29,* 42–43, *42–43,* 148–54, *149–54*
Arum Family, 42, 148
Arum Lily, 148
Arum palaestinum, 152
auricula, 18
Autumn Crocus, 36, 130

B

Baby's Breath, 105
Balamcanda chinensis, 163
barberry, 41
Bearded Iris, 69, 87, *87*
begonia, xvii, 20–25, *20–24,* 62

Hardy, *21,* 23, *23,* 25
Begonia, 20–25, *20–24*
   grandis, 21, 23, *23,* 25, 158
   rex, 23
Begoniaceae, 20–25, *20–24*
Blackberry Lily, *163*
bluebell, *xii, 16–17,* 126, *161*
Boston, *1, 127,* 133
Brooklyn Botanic Garden, *26–27, 33, 40*

C

caladium, xvii, xxiii, 23, *24,* 26–29, *26–29,* 32, 33, 42, 148
   fancyleaved, 29
Caladium, 26–29, *26–29*
   bicolor, 28, 29
   picturatum, 29
   x hortulanum, 26–27, 29, 158
Calla, 148
Calla Lily, *v,* 148, *149–50,* 151–52, *153,* 154, *154, 171*
   'Gigantea', 151
camassia, 68
Canada, *2,* 3, *96*
Canada Lily, 91
Candy Tulip, *139,* 140, 143, 144, *144*
canna, xxiii, 23, 26, *29,* 30–33, *31–33,* 42, 68

'City of Portland', *33*

Common Garden, 32

'Crozy', 32

'Longwood Yellow', *31*

Orchid-flowered, 32

'Pretoria', *29*

Canna, 30–33, *31–33*

  edulis, 30

  flaccida, 32

  indica, 30, 158

  warsewiczii, 32

  x generalis, 32

  x orchiodes, 32

Cannaceae, 30–33, *31–33*

carnation, 18

Caryopteris, *132*

Caryopteris clandonensis, 135

Central Park, New York City, 76, *107*

Chapel Hill, North Carolina, *55*

Charleston, South Carolina, *43*

Charlotte, North Carolina, *xix, 161*

chasmanthe, xxiii, 34–35, *35, 114*

Chasmanthe, 34–35, *35*, 103

  aethiopica, 34, 158

  floribunda, 34

Checkered Lily, 58, *58*, 60

China, 25, 62, 67, 68, 88, 91, 94–97, 100, 113, 114

Chinese Chive, *7, 12, 13*

Chinese Lantern, *84*

Chinese Sacred Lily, xxiii, *35*, 113, *113*, 114, *114*, 115, *171*

Chiondoxa, 122

chive, 6, 7

  Chinese, 7, 12, *13*

chrysanthemum, 20

Chrysanthemum parthenium, 20

Cloisters, New York City, *ii, 8, 37, 39, 54*, 91, *162*

colchicum, 25, 36–41, *36–40*, 84, 125

  Autumn Crocus, 36

  Meadow Saffron, 36

  Naked Boys, xxi, 36, *36*, 100

  Naked Nannies, 36

  Star-naked Boys, 36

Colchicum, 36–41, *36–40*

  autumnale, 38–39, *39*, 41, 100, 158

  speciosum, 39, 41, 158

Cold Spring, New York, *10, 90, 94, 111, 141*

colocasia, xxiii, 26, 28, 32, 33, 42–43, *42–43*, 148

  Elephant's Ear, 28, 33, 42, *42*, 43

  Taro, 28, 43

Colocasia, 42–43, *42–43*

  esculenta, 42, 43, 158

Colonial Williamsburg, Virginia, *14, 19, 142–44*

Common Garden Canna, 32

Connecticut, *3, 66, 95*

Cornish, North Carolina, *64–65*

crocus, xvii, xxiii, *xxiii*, 39, 44–51, *44–50*, 65, 129, 130

  Autumn, 36, 130

  'Charles Dickens', 51

  'David Rizzio', 51

  Dutch, 49

  'Florence Nightingale', 51

  'Lord Palmerston', 51

  'Princess of Wales', 51

  Saffron, 47–48, *164*

  'Sir Walter Scott', 51

Crocus, 44–51, *44–50*

  chrysanthus, 158

  sativus, 47–48, *164*

  speciosus, 48, *48*, 49, *49, 117*, 158

  vernus, 49, 158

Crown Imperial, 58

"Crozy" Canna, 32

Custard Lily, 65

cyclamen, 41, 52–57, *52–57*, 135, *135*

  Florist's, 55

  Sowsbread, 54–55

Cyclamen, 52–57, *52–57*

  coum, 52, 53, 54, 55, 158

  hederifolium, 53, 54, 55, *55*, 57, *57*, 158

persicum, 52, *54,* 55, 158

purpurascens, 54–55, 158

D

daffodil, xvii, xxi, 65, 108–19, *109–19,* 130, *165*

    Hoop Petticoat, *112,* 113

    'King Alfred', xxi, 115, *115,* 116

    see also narcissus

Daffodil Family, 130

dahlia, *xvi,* 18, 77

Davidia involucrata, 95

daylily, xxi, 62–69, *63–69,* 151

    Custard, 65

    Dwarf, 65, 67, 69

    Lemon, *64–65,* 65, 67, 68, 69, 84

    Night-Blooming, 65, 68

    Orange, 62, 67

    Tawny, *63,* 65, 67, 68

    Yellow, *64,* 65–66

delphinium, *86*

dieffenbachia, 28

Dominican Republic, *22, 24*

Dove Tree, 95

Durham, North Carolina, *33, 42*

Dutch Crocus, 49

Dwarf Daylily, 65, 67, 69

E

echinops, *64*

Egyptian Onion, *8,* 9

Elephant's Ear, 28, 33, 42, *42,* 43

Endymion, 126

England, *iv,* 3, *12–13,* 18, 40, 47–48, 65, *79,* 82, 85, 91, 92, 94, 104, *105,* 111, 138, 140, 142, 152, 154, *158*

English Iris, 85, 108

eremurus, 68

Exeter, England, *105*

F

Fairy Bells, 102–103, *102–103*

fancyleaved caladium, 29

Fearrington Village, Pittsboro, North Carolina, 7

Feverfew, 20

Flame Flower, 34

Florist's Anemone, 14

Florist's Cyclamen, 55

forcing bulbs, *ii,* xxiii, *xxv, 44–46,* 49, *50,* 51, *71,* 72, *74,* 75, *102–103,* 106, *106,* 113–15, *113–15,* 116, *145,* 147

France, *xxvi,* 3, 16, 18, *24,* 33, 54–55, 82, 91–92, 136–37, 138

G

fritillaria, 14, 58–61, *58–60*

    Checkered Lily, 58, *58,* 60

    Crown Imperial, 58

Fritillaria, 58–61, *58–60*

    imperialis, 58

    meleagris, 58, *58,* 60

    persica, 59, 60, *60,* 61, 158

Garden Hyacinth, 72, 73

    'Jacques', 72

garlic, 6, 8, 9, 11

    Society, 29

Garrison, New York, 117, *117*

German Iris, 85, 87

gladiolus, 2–3, 20, 68, *159*

Gladiolus, 2–3, 20

    byzantinus, 20

    callianthus, 2, 3

gloriosa lily, 29

Glory-of-the-Snow, 122

Gloucester, Virginia, *109*

Gold-banded Lily, 92, 93

golden poppywort, 96

Grape Hyacinth, 61, 71, 104–107, *104–107*

Greece, 17, 38, 47, 77–78, 81, 88

Guernsey Lily, 98–100
Gypsophila paniculata, 105

H

Hardy Begonia, *21*, 23, *23*, 25
Hawaii, 43
Hemerocallis, 62–69, *63–69*, 151
   citrina, 65, 68, 158
   fulva, *63*, 65, 67, 68, 158
   lilioasphodelus, *64–65*, 65–66, 67, 68,
      69, 84, 159
   minor, 65, 67, 69, 159
Hillsborough, North Carolina, *21*, *53*
Hoop Petticoat Daffodil, *112*, 113
Hudson River Valley, New York, *vi*,
      xiii, *xxiv*
Hunnewell estate, Boston, *1*, *127*
Hunt Arboretum, Chapel Hill, North
      Carolina, *55*, *56*, *131*, *134*, 135,
      135
hyacinth, 14, 18, 65, 70–75, *70–74*
   Garden, 72, 73
   Grape, 61, 71, 104–107, *104–107*
   Roman, xxiii, 70, *70–71*, 72, 73–74,
      75, *103*, *114*, *171*
Hyacinthus, 70–75, *70–74*
   orientalis var. albulus, 70, *70–71*, 72,
      73–74, 75, 159, *171*

I

Iceland Poppy, 69
Indian Shot, 30
Iradiceae, 2–5, *2–5*
Iridaceae, 34–35, *35*, 39, 44–51, *44–50*,
      76–87, *76–87*, 102–103, *102–103*
iris, xvii, xxiii, *xxvi*, 11, 65, 76–87, *76–
      87*, *155*, *158*
   Algerian, 84
   Bearded, 69, 87, *87*
   'Cascade Splendor', 87, *87*
   'Chenedolee', *80*, 87
   English, 85, 108
   'Fra Angelico', 87
   German, 85, 87
   'Gracchus', 87
   'I.M. Gedde', 87, *87*
   Japanese, *84*, 85
   'Momauguin', 87, *87*
   orris, 82, *82*, 83, 85, 87
   'Othello', *81*
   'Rosy Wings', 87, *87*
   Siberian, 68, *82*, *83*, 84
   Spanish, 85
   Stinking, 83–84
   'Victorine', *77*, 87
   Yellow Flag, 78, *79*
Iris, 76–87, *76–87*
   danfordiae, 84, 159

   ensata, *84*, 85, 159
   foetidissima, 83–84, 159
   germanica, 85, 87
   laevigata, 85
   pallida, 69, *82*, 83, 85, 87, 159
   pseudacorus, 78, *79*, 159
   reticulata, 84, 159
   sibirica, 68, *82*, *83*, 84, 159
   unguicularis, 84
   variegata, 85
   x flavescens, 87
   xiphioides, 85, 108, 159
   xiphium, 85
Iris Family, 47
Italy, 16, 55

J

Jack-in-the-pulpit, 148
Japan, 25, 62, 67, 91, 99, 100, 113
Japanese Iris, *84*, 85
jonquil, 108

K

'King Alfred' daffodil, xxi, 115, *115*,
      116, 160

L

Lady Tulip, *139,* 140, 143, 144, *144*
leek, 6, 11, 12
Lemon Lily, *64–65,* 65, 67, 68, 69, 84
Liliaceae, 36–41, *36–40,* 58–61, *58–60,*
   62–69, *63–69,* 70–75, *70–74,* 88–97,
   89–96, 104–107, *104–107,* 122–25,
   123–24, 126–29, *126–28,* 136–47,
   137–47
lilies, *iv, xxiv,* 14, 81, 88–97, *89–96,* 130
   Arum, 148
   Blackberry, *163*
   Calla, 148, *149, 150,* 151–52, *153,* 154,
      154, 171
   Canada, 91
   Chinese Sacred, xxiii, *35,* 113, *113,*
      114, *114,* 115, *171*
   gloriosa, 29
   Gold-banded, 92, 93
   Guernsey, 98–100
   Madonna, 88, *89,* 91, 92
   Regal, 88, 92, 94–95, *95,* 96–97
   Resurrection, 100
   Spider, xxi, 98–101, *99–101*
   Tiger, 92, 94
   Trout, *xxiv*
   Trumpet, 148
   White, 91
   see also daylily

Lilium, 88–97, *89–96*
   auratum, 92, 93, 159
   canadense, 91, 159
   candidum, 88, *89,* 91, 92, 159
   catesbaei, 92
   lancifolium, 92, 94, 159
   philadephicum, 92
   regale, 88, 92, 94–95, *95,* 96–97,
      159
   speciosum, 94
   superbum, 92, 160
Lily Family, *xviii,* 39, 58, 67
Lily Leek, 11–12
Lily-of-the-field, 130
Lily-of-the-valley, *xxv,* 65, 87, 106
Long Island, New York, *xx–xxi, 63, 93,*
   146
Longwood Gardens, Kennett Square,
   Pennsylvania, *31, 132–33,* 135
lupin, 69
Lycoris, 98–101, *99–101,* 151
   radiata, 98–101, *99–101,* 160
   squamigera, 100

M

Madonna Lily, 88, *89,* 91, 92
Magnolia soulangia, 107
Massachusetts, *1, 64, 127*

Meadow Rue, 106
Meadow Saffron, 36
Meconopsis integrifolia, 96
Medusa's Trumpet, 113
Melasphaerula, 102–103, *102–103*
   ramosa, 160
Metropolitan Museum of Art, New
   York City, *ii,* 91
Monticello, *ix,* 34, *35, 70, 113, 114,*
   143
Mother-in-law plant, 28
Mount Etna Lily, 130
Murray Bay, Canada, *2, 96*
Muscari, 71, 104–107, *104–107,*
   126
   armeniacum, 61, 104–107, *104–107,*
      160
   botryoides, 105

N

Naked Boys, xxi, 36, *36*
Naked Lady, 100
Naked Nannies, 36
narcissus, *xvii, xix,* xxi, *50,* 108–19,
   109–19, 137
   Chinese Sacred Lily, xxiii, *35,* 113,
      113, 114, *114,* 115
   Hoop Petticoat Daffodil, *112,* 113

narcissus (cont'd)
  'King Alfred', xxi, 115, *115,* 116, 160
  Paperwhite, xxiii, 113, 114, *117*
  Poet's, *109,* 113
  see also daffodil
Narcissus, 108–19, *109–19*
  autumnalis major, 130
  bulbocodium, 112, 113
  bulbocodium var. *conspicuus, 112,* 113,
    160
  hispanicus, 116
  minimus, 109
  moschatus, 111
  poeticus, 109, 113
  tazetta, 108, 113–15
  tazetta var. *orientalis, 35,* 113, *113,* 114,
    114, 115, 160, *171*
nasturtium, *40,* 41
Nerine sarniensis, 98–100, 151
Netherlands, 98, 104, 138, 140
New Hampshire, *64–65*
New Jersey, *xxv*
New York, *ii, 8, 9, 10,* 11, *13,* 14, *23,*
    37, 64, 76–77, *76–77, 80–81, 83,* 87,
    87, 90, 94, 107, 111, 117, 133, *141,*
    159, 162
Night-Blooming Daylily, 65, 68
North Carolina, *xii, xix,* 7, 9, *21, 29,*
    32–33, 42, 53, 55, 56, 57, 67, 99–
    100, 125, *131, 134,* 135, *135, 161,*
    163, 164

O

Oca, 120
Oenothera missourensis, 25
Old Salem, North Carolina, *164*
onion, *xviii,* 6, 8, *8,* 9, 11, 12
  Egyptian, *8,* 9
  spring, 6
Orange Daylily, 62, 67
Orchid-flowered Canna, 32
Oregon, *84*
orris, 82, *82,* 83, 85, 87
Oxalidaceae, 120–21, *120–21*
oxalis, *103,* 120–21, *120–21*
Oxalis, 120–21, *120–21*
  tuberosa, 120
  versicolor, 120–21, *120–21,* 160

P

pansy, 18
Paperwhite Narcissus, xxiii, 113, 114,
  117
Pennsylvania, *31, 86, 132, 133,* 135
peony, 65, 69, 77
Philadelphia, *86*
Phytolacca americana, 131
pinks, 18

Pittsboro, North Carolina, 7
Poet's Narcissus, *109,* 113
polyanthuses, 18
poppy, *82, 86*
poppywort, 96
primrose, *105*
Primulaceae, 52–57, *52–57*
puschkinia, xxiii, 41, 122–25, *123–24,*
  126
Puschkinia, 122–25, *123–24*
  hyacinthoides, 122
  libanotica, 122
  scilloides, 122, 160
  sicula, 122

Q

Quaker Ladies, *115*
Queensland arrowroot, 30

R

Raleigh, North Carolina, *67*
Ramsons, 12, *12–13*
Ranunculaceae, 14–19, *14–19*
Red Hook, New York, *15*
Regal Lily, 88, 92, 94–95, *95,* 96–97

Resurrection Lily, 100
Rhus typhina 'Laciniata', *83*
Richardia, 148
Roman Hyacinth, xxiii, 70, *70–71*, 72, *73–74*, 75, *103, 114, 171*
'Rosa Mundi', 41
rose, 77
Russia, 122

S

Saffron Crocus, 47–48, *164*
Sanguinaria canedensis, vi
scilla, *1*, 122, 125, 126–29, *126–28*
Scilla, 126–29, *126–28*
  alba, 126
  amoena, 126
  bifolia, 126
  rubra, 126, 128
  sibirica, 126–29, 160
  sibirica var. *atrocoerula*, 129
  sicula, 122
  verna, 126
Sea Onion, 126
Seville, Spain, *153*
Shaftsbury, England, *79*
shallot, 6
Siberian Iris, 68, *82, 83*, 84

Siberian Squill, 126–29, *126–28*
'Spring Beauty', 129
Snowdrop, *xxv*, 129
Society Garlic, 29
Solidago caesia, 135
Somerset, England, *iv, 158*
South America, 23, 30, 32
South Carolina, *43*
Sowsbread, 54–55
Spain, 81, 85, *150, 153*
Spanish Iris, 85
Spider Lily, xxi, 98–101, *99–101*
Spotted Calla, 152
spring onion, 6
Squill, 71
  Siberian, 126–29, *126–28*
  'Spring Beauty' Siberian, 129
  Striped, 122
Staghorn Sumac, *83*
Star-naked Boys, 36
Stars of Persia, *9*, 11
sternbergia, 130–35, *131–35*
Sternbergia, 130–35, *131–35*
  clusiana, 132, 133, *133*, 135, 140, 160
  lutea, 132–33, *134*, 135, *135*, 160
  macrantha, 133

Stinking Iris, 83–84
Striped Squill, 122

T

Taro, 28, 43
  Wild, 28
Tawny Daylily, *63*, 65, 67, 68
Thalictrum minor, 106
Tiger Lily, 92, 94
Tintinbull, Somerset, England, *iv, ix*
Trillium erectum, xiii
Trout Lily, *xxiv*
Trumpet Lily, 148
tuberose, 14, 65
tulip, *xvii*, 14, 65, 136–47, *137–47*
  Candy, *139*, 140, 143, 144, *144*
  Lady, *139*, 140, 143, 144, *144*
  'Macrospila', 144
  'Queen of the Night', *141*
Tulipa, 136–47, *137–47*
  clusiana, 139, 140, 143, 144, *144*, 160, *168*
  dasystemon, 144
  linofolia, 145
  saxatilis, 143, *144*, 145, 147, 160

sylvestris, 106
tarda, 143, 144, *144,* 145,
160
Turkey, 142–43

V

Veronica teucrium, 69
Versailles, *24*
violet, 106
Virginia, *14, 19, 79, 82,* 92, 100,
109, 112, 113, 120, *126, 140,*
142–44, 147, 160,
165

W

Wave Hill, New York, *xvi, 9, 13, 23,*
64, 76–77, *76–77, 80–81, 83,* 87, *87*
White Lily, 91
Wild Taro, 28
Winston-Salem, North Carolina, *164*
Winter Jasmine, 41
Winterthur, *36*
Wood Sorrel, 120, 121

Y

Yellow Daylily, *64,* 65–66

Yellow Flag, 78, *79*
Yellow Tuberose, 65

Z

zantedeschia, 148–54, *149–54*
'Albo-maculata', 152
'Little Gem', 152
Zantedeschia, 148–54, *149–54*
aethiopica, 148, *149, 150,* 151–
52, *153,* 154, *154, 160,*
171
elliottiana, 152
rehmannii, 152

ABOUT THE AUTHOR AND PHOTOGRAPHER

KATHERINE WHITESIDE and MICK HALES, collaborators on the successful *Antique Flowers,* have teamed up for features that have appeared in *HG, Elle Decor, Connoisseur, Garden Design, Landscape Architecture,* and *House Beautiful.* Mick Hales has also contributed photos to *Vanity Fair, Architectural Record,* and many European magazines.

GARDENER'S NOTES

GARDENER'S NOTES

❦

GARDENER'S NOTES